PENGUIN BOOKS

THE A        THEORIST

Paul Krugman was proclaimed by          economist of his generation', a jud          American Economic Association pres          Clark Medal, a prize given every two years to the best American economist under the age of forty. In addition to his research, Krugman writes extensively for general audiences. His book, *Peddling Prosperity*, was hailed by *Newsweek* as 'the best primer around on recent US economic history'. His book *The Return of Depression Economics* was recently published in hardback by Allen Lane The Penguin Press.

# The Accidental Theorist

## And Other Dispatches from the Dismal Science

**Paul Krugman**

PENGUIN BOOKS

## PENGUIN BOOKS

Published by the Penguin Group
Penguin Books Ltd, 80 Strand, London WC2R 0RL, England
Penguin Putnam Inc., 375 Hudson Street, New York, New York 10014, USA
Penguin Books Australia Ltd, 250 Camberwell Road, Camberwell, Victoria 3124, Australia
Penguin Books Canada Ltd, 10 Alcorn Avenue, Toronto, Ontario, Canada M4V 3B2
Penguin Books India (P) Ltd, 11 Community Centre, Panchsheel Park, New Delhi – 110 017, India
Penguin Books (NZ) Ltd, Cnr Rosedale and Airborne Roads, Albany, Auckland, New Zealand
Penguin Books (South Africa) (Pty) Ltd, 24 Sturdee Avenue, Rosebank 2196, South Africa

Penguin Books Ltd, Registered Offices: 80 Strand, London WC2R 0RL, England

www.penguin.com

First published in the USA by W. W. Norton & Company Inc. 1998
First published in Great Britain in Penguin Books 1999
14

Copyright © Paul Krugman, 1999

Printed in England by Clays Ltd, St Ives plc

ISBN-13: 978-0-14-028686-1

www.greenpenguin.co.uk

Penguin Books is committed to a sustainable future
for our business, our readers and our planet.
The book in your hands is made from paper
certified by the Forest Stewardship Council.

# *Contents*

# Introduction

Economists are supposed to be boring. And the reputation is jus-tified: Most of us really *are* quite boring, at least when we talk about our work. But then so are most other people, from scien-tists to supermodels. Why do economists get singled out?

The answer, I believe, is unrequited longing. Economics *matters* to people—it is, as John Maynard Keynes put it, "dangerous for good or evil" in a way that, say, literary studies or even history are not. People come to economists in search of emotional or political satisfaction. They are therefore dismayed to find a discipline that seems to be all equations, diagrams, and impenetrable jargon.

There are some excuses for that impenetrability. Economics, Keynes wrote elsewhere, is "a difficult and technical subject, but nobody will believe it." The central ideas of economic theory are very simple: They boil down to little more than the proposition that people will usually take advantage of opportunities, plus the observation that my opportunities often depend on your actions and vice versa. But applying these ideas to particular cases—to the effects of technological progress on employment, of international trade on wages, of the money supply on economic growth—requires some close, hard thinking, thinking in which a bit of math and some specialized jargon can often help you stay on track. This is not to deny that much of what modern economists (or academics of any type) do is pointless technical showboating, using fancy math to say things that could just as well have been expressed in plain English—or for that matter to say things that would be obviously silly if their meaning were not obscured by the math. But not all of the technicality of modern economics is obscurantism; sometimes it is actually a way to make things clearer and simpler.

Still, there should be a lot more accessible, interesting, even exciting writing about economics than there is. Astronomy is a difficult, technical subject, too; yet where is the economics equivalent of the late Carl Sagan? (Did you know that U.S. consumers spend trillions and trillions . . . never mind.) On many issues, including some of those where passions run highest, economics offers startlingly illuminating insights, insights that could with a little effort (all right, with a *lot* of effort) be explained without the jargon. Yet that explanation is usually not forthcoming. We are a profession without popularizers.

But wait—aren't there some very influential economic gurus, men whose books routinely grace the best-seller lists? Yes, there are, but they are not popularizers in the proper sense of the word. Sagan *was* a popularizer: He found a way to make serious astronomy—the discoveries and theories of professional astronomers—comprehensible and exciting to a wide audience. Our popular economics writers, however, are *not* in the business of giving their readers a ringside seat on the research action; with no exception I can think of, they use their books to do an end run around the normal structure of scholarship, to preach ideas that few serious economists share. Often, these ideas are not just at odds with the professional consensus; they are demonstrably wrong, and sometimes terminally silly. But they sound good to the unwary reader. In fact, as far as most people know—including people who regard themselves as well-informed, who watch public TV and read intellectual magazines—that is what economics sounds like.

The essays in this volume represent attempts to do something about that. For most of my professional life I did what most academics do: I taught my classes, wrote papers for professional journals, and in general talked mainly with other academics. As far as I was concerned, getting at the truth and convincing a select audience of cognoscenti that I was right was all that mattered; it was somebody else's job to communicate that truth to the world at large. To be honest, I would go back to those innocent days if I could; in a way I feel that I have been expelled from Eden. But there is no going back, for I have become all too aware that the truth does not, in fact, always prevail—that plausible charlatans can often convince even the great and good that they are men of wisdom, that economic ideas of (it seems to me) self-evident silliness often sound profound to the untrained ear. And I cannot count on somebody else to make the case for the kind of economics I believe in; if I want that case made, I'll have to do it myself.

Luckily, though it's a tough job, it's not impossible. If you work at it hard enough you can often find a way—a parable, a metaphor, a particular angle of approach—that makes a seemingly abstruse piece of economics easily accessible. And there is also a lot of pleasure, of sheer fun in the craft of writing clear English about a technical subject.

And so a few years ago I found myself launched on a sort of second career, writing the sort of pieces that are collected in this book. Often I write articles that use some current issue as their starting point; I also often try either to explode some plausible-sounding idea that happens to be false or to promote some implausible, disturbing idea that happens to be true. But I always have the additional purpose of demonstrating what it means to think, really think, about economics.

This second career has not always made me popular. Many people have strong ideas about economics, partly because our daily experience of getting and spending gives us a (sometimes false) sense of understanding the larger picture, partly because it is so easy to become convinced by economic doctrines that suit our political prejudices. How do people with such strong ideas react when an economist tells them that some things they thought were obviously true are actually quite false, as false as the folk medicine that says that people get ulcers because they worry too much;[1] and that some ideas that they find distasteful are equally unambiguously true, as true as the theory of evolution by natural selection? Perhaps they should be grateful to be thus enlightened; but for some reason they usually aren't. Moreover, some influential writers and speakers on economics have spent most of their careers, well, faking it: misrepresenting or even inventing facts, using clever rhetoric to cover gaping logical holes. Neither they nor the people who have been taken in by them are particularly happy to see this pointed out. And some people are simply outraged by the suggestion that economics is even potentially a subject in which hard thinking might force them to question their

---

[1] Recent research has shown that the great majority of ulcers are the result of a bacterial infection.

preconceptions—that is, wrote one angry op-ed author, an unfor-
giveable "accusation of illiteracy." This was the attitude Keynes was
referring to when he wrote that while economics is a difficult and
technical subject, "nobody will believe it."

I may as well bring up one particular issue while I am on this
topic. I sometimes find it necessary to name names—to illustrate a
particular bad idea by citing an actual example of a prominent person who espouses that idea. This may look like malice—why get
personal?—but I actually have a serious purpose. All too often, I
have found, the peddlers of economic nonsense play a game of bait
and switch—drawing their audience in with the promise of
sophisticated analysis, then providing instead crudely simplistic
stories. Worse yet, when somebody like me tries to argue against
those simplistic stories, the usual response is "But nobody believes
*that*," followed almost instantly by a reiteration of the same idea,
slightly restated. What's a polemicist to do? Well, it turns out to be
helpful to catch them with their hand in the cookie jar. Partly this
is because I need to prove that real, important people do indeed
hold the views I am criticizing—that I am not attacking straw
men. But I also find that by showing how easy it is to be misled—
to be convinced by an appealing, serious-sounding argument that
can be shown to be nonsense pure and simple—I can convince
my readers that they really do need to listen to what I have to say.
Either that, or send me an abusive letter, an option that quite a few
seem to prefer.

But while I have not always made friends in my second career, I
like to think that I have at least now and then influenced people.

The pieces collected here are adapted from essays written
between the fall of 1995 and the summer of 1997. It was an event-
ful period (but then aren't they all?), and a fertile time for nonsense
both right and left. The earliest piece in the collection was written in response to the mean-spirited nonsense spouted by America's newly elected Republican House majority leader; one of the

latest in response to the warm-hearted but unfortunately equally silly ideas of France's newly elected Socialist prime minister. But anyway, left and right are not adequate categories: On most of the issues touched on in this collection, the orthodoxy of both liberals and conservatives is simply wrong, and in many cases the truth is something nobody wants to hear.

About half of these articles were published in the online magazine *Slate*, where I have a regular monthly column, "The Dismal Science"; most of the rest in such conventional print media as the *Washington Monthly, Foreign Affairs,* and the *New York Times.* A few of the pieces are new to print. Although many were written to some degree in response to current events, I am not a reporter; if I have anything to contribute to discussion of the news, it comes from putting that news in a longer-term context. Thus I hope that readers will find that the pieces have not dated too much, that all of them remain relevant.

Although my ultimate purpose was serious, I enjoyed writing these pieces—even though all the old cliches are absolutely true: It is not only harder but more time-consuming to write a 1,300-word, plain-English article for the general public than to write a 5,000-word, equation-laden paper for a professional journal. I hope some of that enjoyment shows through, that readers find the essays fun as well as enlightening. But try them out and see.

## Part 1

# Jobs, Jobs, Jobs

*A*t the heart of capitalism's inhumanity—and no sensible person will deny that the market is an amoral and often cruelly capricious master—is the fact that it treats labor as a commodity. Economics textbooks may treat the exchange of labor for money as a transaction much like the sale of a bushel of apples, but we all know that in human terms there is a huge difference. A merchant may sell many things, but a worker usually has only one job, which supplies not only his livelihood but often much of his sense of identity. An unsold commodity is a nuisance, an unemployed worker a tragedy; it is terribly unjust that such tragedies are created every day by new technologies, changing tastes, and the ever-shifting flows of world trade. There would be no excuse for an economic system that treats people like objects except that, as Churchill said of democracy, capitalism is the worst system known except all those others that have been tried from time to time. At the end of the twentieth century almost nobody believes that there is any good alternative to a market economy; at best we can hope to cushion people from the worst of that economy's brutalities.

But while almost everyone concedes that, like it or not, most jobs must be supplied by private, self-interested initiative, there is still much confusion about what that concession involves. Part of the problem is that many people are still unwilling to accept the idea that the labor market will not function well unless it is allowed to behave more or less like other markets. But this is not surprising—after all, not many people really understand the logic of markets in any case; they do not understand the process by which supply and demand often (not always) come into balance without any special encouragement. And there is also, I believe, a natural tendency to suppose that on those occasions when the market fails to provide jobs—when, for example, the economy plunges into a recession—the explanation must involve some deep flaw in the system. It is deeply implausible, even offensive, to suggest that the cause of so much suffering can be something as trivial, technical, and fixable as the failure to print enough money. Indeed, there would be no reason to believe such a silly story, except that it happens to be true.

As a result, muddled thinking about the subject of jobs flourishes, in some cases at the highest levels of government. Particularly depressing for anyone who would like to believe in intellectual progress is the reappearance of decades- or even centuries-old fallacies, stated as if they were profound and novel insights—as if those who propound them have transcended conventional views, when in fact they have merely failed to understand them.

The title essay in this collection was an effort to take on an old misunderstanding that has lately experienced a revival of popularity: the idea (sometimes referred to as the "lump of labor" fallacy) that there is only a limited amount of work to be done in the world, and that as productivity rises there is therefore a reduction in the number of jobs available. The idea has a surface plausibility from the experience of individual industries: It is indeed true, for example, that America's railroads handle more freight now than they did in 1980, but employ barely a third as many workers. Doesn't it follow that the same fate may await all jobs, that as workers become more productive the economy will need ever fewer of them? It is hard to explain that this involves a fallacy of composition, that the effect of a productivity increase *in a given industry* on the number of jobs *in that industry* is very different from the effect of a productivity increase *in the economy as a whole* on the *total* number of jobs. In the essay I tried to find a painless way of making that point—and along the way to give readers some idea of what it really means to think about economics, what economic theory really is.

The essay made some use of the fact that despite large productivity gains in some parts of the U.S. economy—and stagnant employment in manufacturing, mainly because of those productivity gains—America has, just as theory would predict, actually done quite well at employing its growing labor force. Yet there was a period in 1995 and 1996 when the headlines were dominated by stories of layoffs, to such an extent that it was hard to remember that despite the prevalence of such stories the U.S. economy was actually creating jobs at a near-record pace. In the second piece, "Downsizing Downsizing," I tried to talk about this gap between perception and reality. (For the record: My remark about "emotionally satisfying fictions" was in the original version, written when Robert Reich was still Labor Secretary.)

While the idea that capitalism suffers from being too productive mainly rests on a naive failure to think the matter through, some commentators who hold this view have managed to convince themselves that they are bold and forward-looking thinkers, drawing their inspiration from that great economist John Maynard Keynes—who must, as I argue in "Vulgar Keynesians," be turning over in his grave.

Of course, some countries *are* having trouble creating jobs. I conclude this section with an essay about the sad case of France: a country in which fashionably muddled thinking has helped to create mass unemployment—and in which the political elite seems determined to draw the wrong lessons from that experience.

# The Accidental Theorist

Imagine an economy that produces only two things: hot dogs and buns. Consumers in this economy insist that every hot dog come with a bun, and vice versa. And labor is the only input to production.

OK, time out. Before we go any further, I need to ask what you think of an essay that begins this way. Does it sound silly to you? Were you about to turn the page, figuring that this couldn't be about anything important?

One of the points of this essay is to illustrate a paradox: You

Originally published in *Slate*, January 23, 1997.

can't do serious economics unless you are willing to be playful. Economic theory is not a collection of dictums laid down by pompous authority figures. Mainly, it is a menagerie of thought experiments—parables, if you like—that are intended to capture the logic of economic processes in a simplified way. In the end, of course, ideas must be tested against the facts. But even to know what facts are relevant, you must play with those ideas in hypothetical settings. And I use the word "play" advisedly: Innovative thinkers, in economics and other disciplines, often have a pronounced whimsical streak. It so happens that I am about to use my hot-dog-and-bun example to talk about technology, jobs, and the future of capitalism. And I plan to make some serious points about those subjects—the kind of points that can only be made if you are willing to play around with a thought experiment or two.

So let's continue. Suppose that our economy initially employs 120 million workers, which corresponds more or less to full employment. It takes two person-days to produce either a hot dog or a bun. (Hey, realism is not the point here.) Assuming that the economy produces what consumers want, it must be producing 30 million hot dogs and 30 million buns each day; 60 million workers will be employed in each sector.

Now, suppose that improved technology allows a worker to produce a hot dog in one day rather than two. And suppose that the economy makes use of this increased productivity to increase consumption to 40 million hot dogs with buns a day. This requires some reallocation of labor, with only 40 million workers now producing hot dogs, 80 million producing buns.

Then a famous journalist arrives on the scene. He takes a look at recent history and declares that something terrible has happened: *Twenty million hot-dog jobs have been destroyed.* When he looks deeper into the matter, he discovers that the output of hot dogs has actually risen 33 percent, yet employment has declined 33 percent. He begins a two-year research project, touring the globe as he talks with executives, government officials, and labor leaders. The picture becomes increasingly clear to him: Supply is growing at a breakneck pace, and there just isn't enough consumer demand to go around. True, jobs are still being created in the bun sector; but soon enough the technological revolution will destroy those jobs, too. Global capitalism, in short, is hurtling toward crisis. He writes up his alarming conclusions in a five-hundred-page book. It is full of startling facts about the changes underway in technology and the global market; larded with phrases in Japanese, German, Chinese, and even Malay; and punctuated with occasional barbed remarks about the blinkered vision of conventional economists. The book is widely acclaimed for its erudition and sophistication, and its author becomes a lion of the talk-show circuit.

Meanwhile, economists are a bit bemused, because they can't quite understand his point. Yes, technological change has led to a shift in the industrial structure of employment. But there has been no net job loss; and there is no reason to expect such a loss in the future. After all, suppose that productivity were to double in buns as well as hot dogs. Why couldn't the economy simply take advantage of that higher productivity to raise consumption to 60 million hot dogs with buns, employing 60 million workers in each sector?

Or, to put it a different way: Productivity growth in one sector can very easily reduce employment *in that sector*. But to suppose that productivity growth reduces employment in the economy *as a whole* is a very different matter. In our hypothetical economy it is—or should be—obvious that reducing the number of workers it takes to make a hot dog reduces the number of jobs in the hot-dog sector but creates an equal number in the bun sector, and vice versa. Of course, you would never learn that from talking to hot-dog producers, no matter how many countries you visit; you might not even learn it from talking to bun manufacturers. It is an insight that you can gain only by playing with hypothetical economies—by engaging in thought experiments.

Is this thought experiment too simple to tell us anything about the real world? No, not at all. For one thing, if for "hot dogs" you substitute "manufactures" and for "buns" you substitute "services," my story actually looks quite a lot like the history of the U.S. economy over the past generation. Between 1970 and the present, the economy's output of manufactures roughly doubled; but, because of increases in productivity, employment actually declined slightly. The production of services also roughly doubled—but there was little productivity improvement, and employment grew by 90 percent. Overall, the U.S. economy added more than 45 million jobs. So in the real economy, as in the parable, productivity growth in one sector seems to have led to job gains in the other.

There is also a deeper point: A simple story is not the same as a simplistic one. Even our little parable reveals possibilities that no amount of investigative reporting could uncover. It suggests, in particular, that what might seem to a naive commentator like a natural conclusion—if productivity growth in the steel industry reduces the number of jobs for steelworkers, then productivity growth in the economy as a whole reduces employment in the economy as a whole—may well involve a crucial fallacy of composition.

But wait—what entitles me to assume that consumer demand will rise enough to absorb all the additional production? One good answer is: Why not? If production were to double, and all that production were to be sold, then total income would double, too; so why wouldn't consumption double? That is, why should there be a shortfall in consumption merely because the economy produces more?

Here again, however, there is a deeper answer. It is possible for economies to suffer from an overall inadequacy of demand—recessions do happen. However, such slumps are essentially monetary—they come about because people try in the aggregate to hold more cash than there actually is in circulation. (That insight is the essence of Keynesian economics.) And they can usually be cured by issuing more money—full stop, end of story. An overall excess of production capacity (compared to what?) has nothing at all to do with it.

Perhaps the biggest objection to my hot-dog parable is that final bit about the famous journalist. Surely, no respected figure would write a whole book on the world economy based on such a transparent fallacy. And even if he did, nobody would take him seriously. But while the hot-dog-and-bun economy is hypothetical, the journalist is not. The inspiration for this essay was *Rolling Stone* reporter William Greider's widely heralded 1997 book, *One World, Ready or Not: The Manic Logic of Global Capitalism*. That book is exactly as I have described it: a massive, panoramic description of the world economy, which piles fact upon fact (some of the crucial facts turn out to be wrong, but that is another issue) in apparent demonstration of the thesis that global supply is outrunning global demand. Alas, all the facts are irrelevant to that thesis; for they amount to no more than the demonstration that there are many industries in which growing productivity and the entry of new producers has led to a loss of traditional jobs—that is, that hot-dog production is up, but hot-dog employment is down. Nobody, it seems, warned Greider that he needed to worry about fallacies of composition, that the logic of the economy as a whole is not the same as the logic of a single market.

I think I know what people like Greider would answer: that while I am talking mere theory, their arguments are based on the evidence. The fact, however, is that the U.S. economy has added forty-five million jobs over the past twenty-five years—far more jobs have been added in the service sector than have been lost in manufacturing. Greider's view, if I understand it, is that this is just a reprieve—that any day now, the whole economy will start looking like the steel industry. But this is a purely theoretical prediction. And such theorizing is all the more speculative and simplistic because he is an accidental theorist, a theorist despite himself—because he and his unwary readers imagine that his conclusions simply emerge from the facts, unaware that they are driven by implicit assumptions that could not survive the light of day.

Of course, neither the general public, nor even most intellectuals, realized what a thoroughly silly book Greider had written. After all, it looked anything but silly—it seemed knowledgeable and encyclopedic, and was written in a tone of high seriousness. It strains credibility to assert the truth, which is that the main lesson one really learns from all those pages is how easy it is for an intelligent, earnest man to trip over his own intellectual shoelaces.

Why did it happen? Part of the answer is that Greider systematically cut himself off from the kind of advice and criticism that could have saved him from himself. His acknowledgments conspicuously did not include any competent economists—not a surprising thing, one supposes, for a man who describes economics as "not really a science so much as a value-laden form of prophecy." But I also suspect that Greider was the victim of his own earnestness. He clearly took his subject (and himself) too seriously to play intellectual games. To test-drive an idea with seemingly trivial thought experiments, with hypothetical stories about simplified economies producing hot dogs and buns, would have been beneath his dignity. And it is precisely because he was so serious that his ideas were so foolish.

# *Downsizing Downsizing*

The Clinton administration isn't particularly mendacious on economic matters—in fact, economic analysis and reporting under Clinton have been unusually scrupulous. But the president has changed his mind about economic policy so often that now his officials sound insincere even when they speak the plain truth. And so I felt a bit sorry for Joseph Stiglitz, the eminent economist who for a time chaired Clinton's Council of Economic Advisers. In the spring of 1996, Stiglitz released a report on the state of

Originally published in *Slate*, June 26, 1996.

the American worker, more or less confirming what most independent economists had already concluded: Workers were not doing as badly as the headlines might have suggested. In particular, the impact of corporate downsizing had been greatly exaggerated.

Stiglitz's report was, to all appearances, a sincere attempt to produce a realistic picture of the American labor market. Yet it was treated by nearly all commentators as a purely political document—an election-year effort to accentuate the positive.

But the commentators had reason for their skepticism. After all, other members of the administration—especially Labor Secretary Robert Reich—had been insistently pushing a very different view. In the world according to Reich, even well-paid American workers have now joined the "anxious classes." They are liable any day to find themselves downsized out of the middle class. And even if they keep their jobs, the fear of being fired has forced them to accept stagnant or declining wages while productivity and profits soar.

Like much of what Reich says, this story was clear, compelling, brilliantly packaged, and mostly wrong. Stiglitz, by contrast, was telling the complicated truth rather than an emotionally satisfying fiction.

To understand why Reich was wrong (about this and most other things), think about the strange case of the missing children. During the early 1980s, sensationalist journalism, combining true-crime stories with garbled statistics, convinced much of the public that America is a nation where vast numbers of children are snatched from their happy families by mysterious strangers every year. TV shows about "stranger abductions" are a media staple to this day. In reality, however, such crimes are rare: about 300 per year in a nation of 260 million. It's not that abductions never happen. They do, and they are terrible things. Nor is the point that the kids are all right: For hundreds of thousands of American children, life is sheer hell. Almost always, however, the people who victimize children are not strangers. For every child kidnapped by a stranger, at least a thousand are sexually abused by family members. But stranger abductions made good copy, and therefore became a public concern out of all proportion to their real importance.

Corporate downsizing is neither as terrible nor as rare as stranger abduction, but the two phenomena share some characteristics. Like stranger abductions, downsizing is a camera-ready tragedy, perfect for media exploitation, that is only a minor part of the real problem.

Stiglitz's report is full of dense statistical analysis making this point, but here's a quick do-it-yourself version. A February 1996 *Newsweek* cover story entitled "Corporate Killers" listed just about every large layoff by a major corporation over the last five years. The number of jobs eliminated by each company appeared in large type next to a photo of the CEO responsible. The article implied that it was describing a national catastrophe. But if you add up all the numbers, the total comes to 370,000. That is less than one worker in 300—a tiny blip in the number of workers who lose or change jobs every year, even in the healthiest economy. And the great majority of downsized workers do find new jobs. Although most end up making less in their new jobs than they did before, only a fraction experience the much-publicized plunge from comfortable middle class to working poor. No wonder Stiglitz found that the destruction of good jobs by greedy corporations is just not an important part of what is happening to the American worker.

The point is that Reich's style of economics—which relies on anecdotes rather than statistics, slogans rather than serious analysis—cannot do justice to the diversity and sheer size of this vast nation. In America anything that can happen, does: Strangers kidnap children; mathematicians become terrorists; executives find themselves flipping hamburgers. The important question is not whether these stories are true; it is whether they are typical. How do they fit into the big picture?

Well, the big picture looks like this: Both the number of "good jobs" and the pay that goes with those jobs are steadily rising. The workers who have the skill, talent, and luck to get these jobs generally do very well. Only a relative handful of "good job" holders (which is to say only a few hundred thousand a year) experience serious reverses. America's middle class may be anxious, but objectively, it is doing fine.

The people who are really doing badly are those who do not have good jobs and never did. Those with lousy jobs have seen their already-low wages slowly but steadily sink. In other words, the main victims of (to use another of Reich's phrases) the "new economy" are not the few thousand managers who have become hamburger flippers but the tens of millions of hamburger flippers, janitors, and so on whose real wages have been declining 1 or 2 percent per year for the last two decades.

Does this distinction matter? It does if you are trying to set any sort of policy priorities. Should we, as some in the administration wanted, focus our attention on preserving the jobs of well-paid employees at big corporations? Should we pressure those companies to stop announcing layoffs? Should we use the tax system to penalize companies that fire workers and reward those that do not? Or, instead, should we fight tooth and nail to preserve and extend programs like the Earned Income Tax Credit that help the working poor? It is disingenuous to say we should do both: Money is scarce and so is political capital. If we focus on small problems that make headlines, we will ignore bigger problems that don't.

So let's give Joe Stiglitz some credit. No doubt his political masters allowed him to downsize the issue of downsizing at least partly because they believed that good news reelects presidents. Sometimes, however, an economic analysis that is politically convenient also happens to be the honest truth.

# *Vulgar Keynesians*

Economics, like all intellectual enterprises, is subject to the law of diminishing disciples. A great innovator is entitled to some poetic license. If his ideas are at first somewhat rough, if he exaggerates the discontinuity between his vision and what came before, no matter: Polish and perspective can come in due course. But inevitably there are those who follow the letter of the innovator's ideas but misunderstand their spirit, who are more dogmatic in their radicalism than the orthodox were in their orthodoxy. And as ideas

Originally published in *Slate*, February 6, 1997.

spread, they become increasingly simplistic—until what eventually becomes part of the public consciousness, part of what "everyone knows," is no more than a crude caricature of the original.

Such has been the fate of Keynesian economics. John Maynard Keynes himself was a magnificently subtle and innovative thinker. Yet one of his unfortunate if unintentional legacies was a style of thought—call it vulgar Keynesianism—that confuses and befogs economic debate to this day.

Before the 1936 publication of Keynes's *The General Theory of Employment, Interest, and Money*, economists had developed a rich and insightful theory of *microeconomics*, of the behavior of individual markets and the allocation of resources among them. But *macroeconomics*—the study of economy-wide events like inflation and deflation, booms and slumps—was in a state of arrested development that left it utterly incapable of making sense of the Great Depression.

So-called "classical" macroeconomics asserted that the economy had a long-run tendency to return to full employment, and focused only on that long run. Its two main tenets were the quantity theory of money—the assertion that the overall level of prices was proportional to the quantity of money in circulation—and the "loanable funds" theory of interest, which asserted that interest rates would rise or fall to equate total savings with total investment.

Keynes was willing to concede that in some sufficiently long run, these theories might indeed be valid; but, as he memorably pointed out, "In the long run we are all dead." In the short run, he asserted, interest rates were determined not by the balance between savings and investment at full employment but by "liquidity preference"—the public's desire to hold cash unless offered a sufficient incentive to invest in less safe and convenient assets. Savings and investment were still necessarily equal; but if desired savings at full employment turned out to exceed desired investment, what would fall would be not interest rates but the level of employment and output. In particular, if investment demand should fall for whatever reason—such as, say, a stock-market crash—the result would be an economy-wide slump.

It was a brilliant reimagining of the way the economy worked, one that received quick acceptance from the brightest young economists of the time. True, some realized very early that Keynes's picture was oversimplified; in particular, that the level of employment and output would normally feed back to interest rates, and that this might make a lot of difference. Still, for a number of years after the publication of *The General Theory*, many economic theorists were fascinated by the implications of that picture, which seemed to take us into a looking-glass world in which virtue was punished and self-indulgence rewarded.

Consider, for example, the "paradox of thrift." Suppose that for some reason the savings rate—the fraction of income not spent—goes up. According to the early Keynesian models, this will actually lead to a decline in total savings and investment. Why? Because higher desired savings will lead to an economic slump, which will reduce income and also reduce investment demand; since in the end savings and investment are always equal, the total volume of savings must actually fall!

Or consider the "widow's cruse" theory of wages and employment (named after an old folk tale). You might think that raising wages would reduce the demand for labor; but some early Keynesians argued that redistributing income from profits to wages would raise consumption demand, because workers save less than capitalists (actually they don't, but that's another story), and therefore increase output and employment.

Such paradoxes are still fun to contemplate; they still appear in some freshman economics textbooks. Nonetheless, few economists take them seriously these days. There are a number of reasons, but the most important can be stated in two words: Alan Greenspan.

After all, the simple Keynesian story is one in which interest rates are independent of the level of employment and output. But in reality the Federal Reserve Board actively manages interest rates, pushing them down when it thinks employment is too low and raising them when it thinks the economy is overheating. You may quarrel with the Fed chairman's judgment—you may think that he should keep the economy on a looser rein—but you can hardly dispute his power. Indeed, if you want a simple model for predicting the unemployment rate in the United States over the next few years, here it is: It will be what Greenspan wants it to be, plus or minus a random error reflecting the fact that he is not quite God.

But putting Greenspan (or his successor) into the picture restores much of the classical vision of the macroeconomy. Instead of an invisible hand pushing the economy toward full employment in some unspecified long run, we have the visible hand of the Fed pushing us toward its estimate of the noninflationary unemployment rate over the course of two or three years. To accomplish this, the board must raise or lower interest rates to bring savings and investment at that target unemployment rate in line with each other. And so all the paradoxes of thrift, widow's cruses, and so on become irrelevant. In particular, an increase in the savings rate will translate into higher investment after all, because the Fed will make sure that it does.

To me, at least, the idea that changes in demand will normally be offset by Fed policy—so that they will, on average, have no effect on employment—seems both simple and entirely reasonable. Yet it is clear that very few people outside the world of academic economics think about things that way. For example, the debate over the North American Free Trade Agreement was conducted almost entirely in terms of supposed job creation or destruction. The obvious (to me) point that the average unemployment rate over the next ten years will be what the Fed wants it to be, regardless of the U.S.-Mexico trade balance, never made it into the public consciousness. (In fact, when I made that argument at one panel discussion in 1993, a fellow panelist—a NAFTA advocate, as it happens—exploded in rage: "It's remarks like that that make people hate economists!")

What has made it into the public consciousness—including, alas, that of many policy intellectuals who imagine themselves well informed—is a sort of caricature Keynesianism, the hallmark of which is an uncritical acceptance of the idea that reduced consumer spending is always a bad thing. In the United States, where inflation and the budget deficit have receded for the time being, vulgar Keynesianism has recently staged an impressive comeback. The paradox of thrift and the widow's cruse are both major themes in William Greider's latest book, discussed in the first essay. (Although it is doubtful whether he is aware of the source of his ideas—as Keynes wrote, "Practical men, who believe themselves quite exempt from any intellectual influence, are usually the slaves of some defunct economist.") It is perhaps not surprising that the same ideas are echoed in places like the *New Republic*; but when you see the idea that higher savings will actually reduce growth treated seriously in *BusinessWeek* you realize that there is a real cultural phenomenon developing.

To justify the claim that savings are actually bad for growth (as opposed to the quite different, more reasonable position that they are not as crucial as some would claim), you must convincingly argue that the Fed is impotent—that it cannot, by lowering interest rates, ensure that an increase in desired savings gets translated into higher investment.

It is not enough to argue that interest rates are only one of several influences on investment. That is like saying that my pressure on the gas pedal is only one of many influences on the speed of my car. So what? I am able to adjust that pressure, and so the cop who pulls me over for speeding will not normally accept the fact that I was going downhill as an excuse. Similarly, Greenspan is able to change interest rates freely (the Fed can double the money supply in a day, if it wants to), and so the level of employment is normally determined by how high he thinks it can safely go—end of story.

No, to make sense of the claim that savings are bad you must argue either that interest rates have no effect on spending (try telling that to the National Association of Homebuilders) or that potential savings are so high compared with investment opportunities that the Fed cannot bring the two in line even at a near-zero interest rate. The latter was a reasonable position during the 1930s, when the rate on Treasury bills was less than one-tenth of 1 percent; it is an arguable claim right now for Japan, where interest rates are about 1 percent. (Actually, I think that the Bank of Japan could still pull that economy out of its funk, and that its passivity is a case of gross malfeasance. That, however, is a subject for another essay ["What Is Wrong with Japan?"].) But the bank that holds a mortgage on my house sends me a little notice each month assuring me that the interest rate in America is still quite positive, thank you. Anyway, this is a moot point, because the people who insist that savings are bad do not think that the Fed is impotent. On the contrary, they are generally the same people who insist that the disappointing performance of the U.S. economy over the past generation is all the Fed's fault, and that we could grow our way out of our troubles if only Greenspan would let us.

The story seems to go like this: Increasing savings will slow the economy—presumably because the Fed cannot induce an increase in investment by cutting interest rates. Instead, the Fed should stimulate growth by cutting interest rates, which will work because lower interest rates will induce an increase in investment.

Am I missing something?

# Unmitigated Gauls:
## Liberté, Egalité, Inanité

Fifteen years ago, just after François Mitterrand became president of France, I attended my first conference in Paris. I can't remember a thing about the conference itself, although my impressions of the food and wine—this was my first adult visit to the city—remain vivid. The only thing I do remember is a conversation over dinner (*canard aux olives*) with an adviser to the new government, who explained its plan to stimulate the economy with public spending while raising wages and maintaining a strong franc.

Originally published in *Slate*, June 5, 1997.

To the Americans present this program sounded a bit, well, inconsistent. Wouldn't it, we asked him, be a recipe for a balance-of-payments crisis (which duly materialized a few months later)? "That's the trouble with you Anglo-Saxon economists—you're too wrapped up in your theories. You need to adopt a historical point of view." Some of us did, in fact, know a little history. Wasn't the plan eerily reminiscent of the failed program of Léon Blum's 1936 government? "Oh no, what we are doing is completely unprecedented."

The French have no monopoly on intellectual pretensions, or on muddled thinking. They may not even be more likely than other people to combine the two. There is, however, something special about the way the French political class discusses economics. In no other advanced country is the elite so willing to let fine phrases overrule hard thinking, to reject the lessons of experience in favor of delusions of grandeur.

To an Anglo-Saxon economist, France's current problems do not seem particularly mysterious. Jobs in France are like apartments in New York City: Those who provide them are subject to detailed regulation by a government that is very solicitous of their occupants. A French employer must pay his workers well and provide generous benefits, and it is almost as hard to fire those workers as it is to evict a New York tenant. New York's pro-tenant policies have produced very good deals for some people, but they have also made it very hard for newcomers to find a place to live. France's policies have produced nice work if you can get it. But many people, especially the young, can't get it. And, given the generosity of unemployment benefits, many don't even try.

True, some problems are easy to diagnose but hard to deal with. If George Pataki can't end rent control, why should we expect Jacques Chirac to cure Eurosclerosis? But what is mysterious about France is that as far as one can tell, absolutely nobody of consequence accepts the obvious diagnosis. On the contrary, there seems to be an emerging consensus that what France needs is—guess what?—more regulation. Socialist leader (and now prime minister) Lionel Jospin's idea of a pro-employment policy is to require employers to pay workers the same money for fewer hours. Even conservative leader Philippe Séguin, regarded as an iconoclast by French standards because he has questioned the sacred goal of European monetary union, thinks that one way to add jobs is to ban self-service pumps at gas stations.

Beyond more of the same, what does the French elite see as the answer to the nation's problems? For more than a decade its members have sought salvation in the idea of Europe—that is, a unified European economy (under French leadership, of course), with common regulations and a common currency. In such a continental market, they imagine, France can once again prosper.

Now a unified European market is a pretty good idea. There is even a reasonable case for unifying Europe's currencies—although there is also a good case for doing no such thing. (There is a whole industry of people—eurologists?—who make a living by debating that issue.) But to acknowledge the potential virtues of European economic integration risks missing the essential fatuousness of the whole project. France's problem is unemployment (currently almost 13 percent). Nothing else is even remotely as important. And whatever a unified market and a common currency may or may not achieve, they will do almost nothing to create jobs. Think of it this way: Imagine that several cities, all suffering housing shortages because of rent control, agree to make it easier for landlords in one city to own buildings in another. This is not a bad idea. It might even slightly increase the supply of apartments. But it is not going to get at the heart of the problem. Yet all the grand schemes for European integration amount to no more than that.

Indeed, in practice, the dream of European unity has actually made things worse. If you are going to have a common currency, everything we know suggests you should follow what Berkeley's

Barry Eichengreen calls the Nike strategy. But instead of just doing it, European nations agreed to a seven-year transition period during which they would be required to meet a complex set of criteria—mainly to reduce their budget deficits while keeping their currencies strong.

There is nothing wrong with balancing your budget. In fact, European nations need to do some serious fiscal housecleaning. And as the happy experience of America under Bill Clinton has shown, it is quite possible to reduce the deficit and increase employment at the same time. All you need to do is cut interest rates, so that private spending takes up the slack. But you can't cut interest rates if you are obliged to keep your currency strong. So the Maastricht Treaty (the blueprint for European currency union) ensured that the budget-cutting it required would be all pain and no gain. Nobody can make a precise estimate, but a guess is that without Maastricht, France's unemployment rate might be two or three percentage points lower than it is.

While some French politicians have been willing to say nice things about budget deficits, however, nobody seems willing to challenge the dogma that European integration is the answer. Even Séguin the iconoclast declares that "the fight against unemployment is inseparable from the realization of the grand European design." But let us not blame French politicians. Their inanities only reflect the broader tone of economic debate in a nation prepared to blame its problems on everything but the obvious causes. France, say its best-selling authors and most popular talking heads, is the victim of globalization—although adroit use of red tape has held imports from low-wage countries to a level far below that in the United States (or Britain, where the unemployment rate is now only half that of France). France, they say, is the victim of savage, unrestrained capitalism—although it has the largest government and the smallest private sector of any large advanced country. France, they say, is the victim of currency speculators, whose ravages President Chirac once likened to those of AIDS.

The refusal of the French elite to face up to what looks like reality to the rest of us may doom the very European dreams that have sustained the nation's illusions. After this last election it is clear that the French will not be willing to submit to serious fiscal discipline. Will the Germans still be willing to give up their beloved deutsche mark in favor of a currency partly managed by France? It is equally clear that France will not give up its taste for regulation—indeed, it will surely try to impose that taste on its more market-oriented neighbors, especially Britain. That will give those neighbors—yes, even Tony Blair—plenty of reason to hesitate before forming a closer European Union.

But if it turns out that Chirac's political debacle is the beginning of a much larger disaster—the collapse of the whole vision of European glory that has obsessed France for so long—we can be sure of one thing: The French will blame it all on someone else.

# Right-Wing
# Wrongs

*S*ome of my friends tell me that I should spend more time attacking right-wingers. After all, while the economic nonsense of the right may be no worse than that of the left, it is a fact of life that any idea appealing to the prejudices and interests of the wealthy is guaranteed a powerful constituency. Supply-side economics is a crank doctrine pure and simple, yet it has been the official ideology of the Republican party for seventeen years.

The problem is finding things to say. Supply-siders never tire of proclaiming that taxes are the root of all evil, but reasonable people do get tired of explaining, over and over again, that they aren't. My personal experience is that once you have stated the main case against supply-side economics a few times, diminishing returns set in; after that you must find other angles of approach.

One such angle, of course, is to ask why anybody believes this stuff in the first place; I begin here with an essay called "The Virus Strikes Again," originally written just after Bob Dole's presidential campaign decided to run on a supply-side platform.

Another apparent opportunity to say something useful about supply-side economics came in the summer of 1997, when even conservatives found themselves asking how the remarkable prosperity of the economy could be reconciled with the grim warnings of their ideologues only a few years earlier. In fact, the new op-ed page editor of the *Wall Street Journal* commissioned me to write a piece on the subject, which I duly did. What was he thinking? For that matter, what was I thinking? As surely as night follows day, the supply-sider editor, Robert Bartley, intervened to kill the piece, accusing me of "intellectual dishonesty." Anyway, the piece is published for the first time here as "Supply Side's Silly Season."

Supply-siders are actually most interesting (and self-revealing) when they talk about subjects other than the miraculous effects of tax cuts. It is illuminating, for example, to see how they deal with uncomfortable realities. The third essay here, "An Unequal Exchange," looks at the contortions that the House majority leader—a former economics professor—is willing to go through in an effort to deny the plain fact that America's income distribution has become much more unequal in the last twenty years. "The Lost Fig Leaf" is about another piece of conservative mythology, the belief in a thoroughly false picture of what the government actually does with taxpayers' money. The final essay is about the near-mystical devotion of some conservatives to the gold standard.

# The Virus Strikes Again

Within a few days of presidential candidate Bob Dole's announcement of an economic plan that relied on the magic of supply-side tax cuts, hundreds of articles were published explaining why the plan wouldn't work. And there were hundreds more explaining why Dole, whose contempt for people who believe in that kind of magic is a matter of public record, nonetheless chose to accept their program—and chose one of the most prominent believers as his running mate. I have nothing to add to all of that. But it seems

Originally published in *Slate*, August 15, 1996.

to me that the success of the tax cutters in taking over yet another presidential campaign requires a deeper explanation. Why does supply-side economics have such durability?

It should go without saying that the supply-side idea—which is that tax cuts have such a positive effect on the economy that one need not worry about paying for them with spending cuts—does not persist because of any actual evidence in its favor. If you want, any nonpartisan economist can explain to you at length what really happened during the Reagan years, and why you can't seriously claim his record as an advertisement for supply-side policies. But surely it is enough to look at the extraordinary recent record of the supply-siders as economic forecasters. In 1993, after the Clinton administration had pushed through an increase in taxes on upper-income families, the very same people who have persuaded Dole to run on a tax-cut platform were very sure about what would happen. Newt Gingrich confidently predicted a severe recession. Articles in *Forbes* magazine urged readers to get out of the stock market to avoid the inevitable crash. The *Wall Street Journal* editorial page had no doubts that the tax increase would sharply increase the deficit instead of reducing it. Sure enough, over the next few years the economy created millions of new jobs, the market started setting new records almost every day, and the deficit withered away. I'm not saying that Clinton's policies led to that result—they accounted for only part of the good news about the deficit, and hardly any of the rest. But the point is that the supply-siders were absolutely sure that his policies would produce disaster—and indeed, if their doctrine had any truth to it, they would have.

Nor, I would argue, do supply-side views spread because they are good politics. True, Ronald Reagan won on a supply-side platform—but one suspects he would have won on almost any platform, and that the taunts of "voodoo economics" actually cost him some votes. Today, the supply-side label is a clear liability. Even promoters of the concept shy away from the label. In 1994, Republican leaders like Gingrich and Dick Armey chose to conceal the extent of their tax-cutting fervor from the voters, who they judged would not trust an economic program based on supply-side assumptions. And the word was that even Republican focus groups—the same groups that were used to craft the Contract with America reacted scornfully to the idea of an election-year tax-cut promise. So why does the supply-side idea keep on resurfacing? Probably because of two key attributes that it shares with certain other doctrines, like belief in the gold standard: It appeals to the prejudices of extremely rich men, and it offers self-esteem to the intellectually insecure.

The support of rich men is not a small matter. Despite its centrality to political debate, economic research is a very low-budget affair. The entire annual economics budget at the National Science Foundation is less than twenty million dollars. What this means is that even a handful of wealthy cranks can support an impressive-looking array of think tanks, research institutes, foundations, and so on devoted to promoting an economic doctrine they like. (The role of a few key funders, like the Coors and Olin foundations, in building an intellectual facade for late twentieth-century conservatism is a story that somebody needs to write.) The economists these institutions can attract are not exactly the best and the brightest. Supply-side guru Jude Wanniski has lately been reduced to employing followers of Lyndon LaRouche. But who needs brilliant, or even competent, researchers when you already know all the answers?

The appeal to the intellectually insecure is also more important than it might seem. Because economics touches so much of life, everyone wants to have an opinion. Yet the kind of economics covered in the textbooks is a technical subject that many people find hard to follow. How reassuring, then, to be told that it is all irrelevant—that all you really need to know are a few simple ideas! Quite a few supply-siders have created for themselves a wonderful alternative intellectual history in which John Maynard Keynes was a fraud, Paul Samuelson and even Milton Friedman are fools, and the true line of deep economic thought runs from Adam Smith through obscure turn-of-the-century Austrians straight to them.

And so it doesn't really matter whether supply-side economics makes any sense, or even whether it goes down to a crushing electoral defeat. The supply-siders will always have a safe haven in the world of Free Enterprise Institutes and Centers for the Study of Capitalism, outlets for their views in the pages of *Forbes* and the *Wall Street Journal*, and new recruits who never tire of saying the same things again and again. When I was younger I thought that ridicule could eventually bring the whole farce to an end, but now I know better. For once the political pundits were right: Dole's desperate ploy failed. But while that was the end of him, the supply-siders will be back.

Biologist Richard Dawkins has argued famously that ideas spread from mind to mind much as viruses spread from host to host. It's an exhilaratingly cynical view, because it suggests that to succeed, an idea need not be true or even useful, as long as it has what it takes to propagate itself. (A religious faith that disposes its believers to become martyrs may be quite false, and lethal to its adherents, yet persist if each martyr inspires others.) Supply-side economics, then, is like one of those African viruses that, however often it may be eradicated from the settled areas, is always out there in the bush, waiting for new victims. I had expected Bob Dole, with his worldliness and sharp wit, to have stronger immunity than most. But weakness in the polls made him vulnerable, and he will never recover.

# Supply-Side's Silly Season

Sometimes you have to give points for sheer *chutzpah*. I can't help admiring the fortitude of veteran supply-sider Paul Craig Roberts—who recently declared in his *BusinessWeek* column that the prosperity of the American economy under Bill Clinton proves the validity of, yes, supply-side economics. After all, back in 1993 Roberts, in lockstep with other supply-siders, predicted nothing but disaster from Clintonomics: "a bigger deficit, higher unemployment, rising inflation, and a currency crisis to boot." Faced with the reality of a Dow near 8,000, the lowest unemployment rate in a generation, and the smallest deficit since, well, Ronald

Reagan's first budget, some people would have tried to change the subject. Roberts, however, is made of sterner stuff.

But then, what choice did he have? The standard (and true) riposte to Clintonian triumphalism is that Clinton presides over a prosperity he did not create, that the credit for the good news belongs partly to Alan Greenspan but mainly to the resilience and flexibility of America's private sector. This escape route is not, however, available to supply-siders. If they concede that six years and counting of noninflationary growth in the nineties have had little if anything to do with the policies of Bill Clinton, they can hardly avoid the implication that seven years of expansion during the eighties may have had equally little to do with the policies of Ronald Reagan. And the legend of Reaganomics—which is gradually losing its magic anyway as "morning in America" recedes ever further into the mists, while the debts Reagan left us remain—is about all the supply-siders have left.

What is supply-side economics? It is not, as some of its apologists would have it, simply the recognition that the supply side of the economy matters; one would be hard-pressed to find a card-carrying economist who disagrees with that proposition. Nor is there anything distinctive about the recognition that high marginal tax rates can hurt economic growth—this, too, is an utterly conventional insight. For example, the effect of taxes on savings, investment, and growth was a central preoccupation of the youthful research of Deputy Treasury Secretary Lawrence Summers. Yet Summers is not now and has never been a supply-sider—because he has always thought that other things matter, too.

What defines supply-side economics, in other words, is not what it includes but what it excludes. Supply-siders believe that *only* the supply side matters. You may think that a recession has something to do with inadequate demand, and that the Fed can help jump-start a recovery by cutting interest rates; but supply-siders, at least when they are being consistent, do not (although in practice they have been known to blame the Fed when things go wrong). And they believe not only that taxes affect growth, but that virtually all bad things that happen to the economy are the result of tax increases, all good things the result of tax reductions. The implication of these views, of course, is that supply-siders think that tax cuts are always a good idea—whatever the state of the economy or the government's budget outlook.

This may sound too good to be true, and it is. But for many years now supply-siders have had a stock answer for skeptics: the economic recovery that followed Reagan's tax cuts, which supposedly proved conventional economics wrong and supply-side economics right.

This was always a disingenuous claim, since the events of the 1980s played out according to a thoroughly conventional script. Try, for example, checking out the scenario for disinflation presented in the best-selling mainstream macroeconomics textbook of the late 1970s, by Rudiger Dornbusch and Stanley Fischer: It shows an initial sharp rise in unemployment, followed by a prolonged period of growth during which inflation and unemployment decline together. In other words, the scenario looks pretty much like the actual path of the U.S. economy from 1979 to 1990. But most people have only a vague idea of what conventional economics actually says, and anyway it is hard to argue with success; so for a long time the supply-side movement was able to get away with a misrepresentation both of what actually happened in the eighties and of what it said about the way the world works.

To deny that the experience of the last few years represents a debacle for supply-side ideas, however, requires a heroic act of selective memory. The truth is that supply-siders went very far out on a limb, and that limb came crashing down. Never mind politics: Suppose that you had managed your personal finances based on what you heard four years ago from Newt Gingrich, read in *Forbes*, or for that matter saw on this very page. You would have sold all your stocks, and probably put your money into gold. If the supply-siders were fund managers, not only would you have fired them, you would have sued them for lack of due diligence.

Indeed, you have to turn to Marxism to find a forecasting fiasco on the same scale. Economists often make bad predictions. But it is one thing to fail to predict something hardly anyone else predicts: Most economists didn't see the stagflation of the 1970s coming, but who did? It is something quite different to make a firm prediction, deeply rooted in your ideology—a prediction that is totally at odds with what mainstream economists say, and accompanied by frequent denunciations of those who disagree with you as knaves and fools—and then to get it completely wrong while the mainstream gets it mostly right. That, one might expect, would make it hard for people to take you seriously ever again. Supply-siders said that Clinton's tax increase would cause disaster; conventional economists said it wouldn't. What do you think happened?

But of course supply-side economics will not vanish in a puff of smoke. Economic fallacies never die—at best, they slowly fade away. Human nature being what it is, it is too much to expect someone whose career or sense of self-worth is based on his identification with some doctrine to abandon that doctrine merely because it has been falsified by events. Moreover, any ideology whose main policy prescription is lower taxes on the rich is likely to have extra staying power: Those who preach it are not going to have trouble putting bread on the table. The supply-siders will be with us for a long time to come.

It may be that the spectacular failure of their predictions has contributed to the eccentricity of some recent supply-side pronouncements. It seemed strange when Jack Kemp claimed (during his debate with Al Gore) that he could double the economy's size in fifteen years—that is, achieve fifteen years of 5 percent growth, starting from near-full employment. He must think that Ronald

Reagan, who started with double-digit unemployment yet managed only seven years at less than 4 percent, was an economic wimp. It seems even stranger that Jude Wanniski, who can lay as good a claim as anyone to being the doctrine's creator—and remains inseparable from Kemp—insists that despite all appearances the rich have actually become impoverished. Stock prices, you see, are still lower than they were thirty years ago—if you measure them in gold.

But we should never be surprised when prominent people say foolish things about economics. The history of economic doctrines teaches us that the influence of an idea may have nothing to do with its quality—that an ideology can attract a devoted following, even come to control the corridors of power, without a shred of logic or evidence in its favor. Supply-side economics may have had a meteoric career in the world of politics, but it never did make any sense. And failure may have brought out the silly streak in some supply-siders, but they have not suddenly become cranks. They always were.

# An Unequal Exchange

To a naive reader, Edward N. Wolff's *Top Heavy: A Study of the Increasing Inequality of Wealth in America* might seem unlikely to provoke strong emotional reactions. Wolff, a professor of economics at New York University, provides a rather dry, matter-of-fact summary of trends in wealth distribution, followed by a low-key case for a modest wealth tax. Although Wolff has done a commendable technical job in combining data from a number of sources to produce a fuller picture—in particular, his book tells us

Originally published in *Washington Monthly*, October 1995.

more about both long-term trends and international comparisons than has previously been available—the rough outlines of this story have been familiar and uncontroversial among economists for at least the past five years.

And yet Wolff's book was the target of an astonishing barrage of conservative attacks: multiple op-eds in the *Wall Street Journal*, hostile book reviews, and so on. Why should such a mild-mannered little volume provoke such rage?

The answer is that this is a subject on which many conservatives are unable to hold a rational discussion. Make a mere statement of fact—say, for example, that the top 20 percent of households in the United States own 85 percent of the marketable wealth—and conservatives will insist that you rephrase it as "20 percent of the households have *created* 85 percent of the wealth." Try to assess long-term trends in income distribution using the standard, apolitical device of comparing incomes at the same stage of successive business cycles, such as 1973 and 1989, and you will be accused of an outrageous attempt to distort Ronald Reagan's record by mixing in the Carter years.

Conservatives are wrong about wealth inequality, but they are not irrational. There is a method and political purpose to their maddened reaction—a determination to deny the facts that is dramatically illustrated by House majority leader Richard Armey's new book, *The Freedom Revolution*. Put simply, conservatives don't want the public to know too much because they fear it would hurt them politically.

To understand the significance of Wolff's book, consider this simple parable: There are two societies. In one, everyone makes a living at some occupation—say, fishing—in which the amount people earn over the course of a year is fairly closely determined by their skill and effort. Incomes will not be equal in this society—some people are better at fishing than others, some people are willing to work harder than others—but the range of incomes will not be that wide. And there will be a sense that those who catch a lot of fish have earned their success.

In the other society, the main source of income is gold prospecting. A few find rich mother lodes and become wealthy. Others find smaller deposits, and many find themselves working hard for very little reward. The result will be a very unequal distribution of income. Some of this will still reflect effort and skill: Those who are especially alert to signs of gold, or willing to put in longer hours prospecting, will on average do better than those who are not. But there will be many skilled, industrious prospectors who do not get rich and a few who become immensely so.

Surely the great majority of Americans, no matter how conservative, instinctively feel that a nation that resembles the second imaginary society is a worse place than one that resembles the first. Yet there is also no question that our nation today is much less like the benign society of fishermen—and much more like the harsh society of prospectors—than it was a generation ago. The evidence is overwhelming, and it comes from many sources—from government agencies like the Bureau of the Census, from *Fortune*'s annual survey of executive compensation, and so on. And, of course, there's the evidence that confronts anyone with open eyes. Tom Wolfe is neither an economist nor a liberal, but he is an acute observer. When he wanted to portray what was happening in American society he came up with the world of *The Bonfire of the Vanities*.

Here's a rough (and reasonably certain) picture of what has happened: The standard of living of the poorest 10 percent of American families is significantly lower today than it was a generation ago. Families in the middle are, at best, slightly better off. Only the wealthiest 20 percent of Americans have achieved income growth at anything like the rates nearly everyone experienced between the forties and early seventies. Meanwhile, the income of families high in the distribution has risen dramatically, with something like a doubling of the real incomes of the top 1 percent.

These widening disparities are often attributed to the increasing importance of education. But while it's true that, on average, workers with a college education have done better than those without, the bulk of the divergence has been among those with similar levels of education. High-school teachers have not done as badly as janitors but they have fallen dramatically behind corporate CEOs, even though they have about the same amount of education.

Also, the growth of inequality cannot be described simply as the rise of some group, such as the college educated or the top 20 percent, compared with the rest; the top 5 percent have gotten richer compared with the next 15, the top 1 percent compared with the next 4, the top 0.25 percent compared with the next 0.75, and onwards all the way to Bill Gates. The important contribution of Wolff's book is that it reinforces the evidence that much of the important action in American inequality has taken place way up the scale, among the extremely well-off.

Wolff focuses on wealth rather than income—on assets rather than cash flow. This has some advantages over annual income as an indicator of a family's economic position, especially among the rich. Someone with a very high income may be having an unusually good year, while it is not unheard of for wealthy families to have negative income if they make a bad investment; in each case their assets will be a better clue to where they really fit in the rankings. More important, however, wealth is in some ways a better indicator than income data of what is happening to the very successful—simply because it is so narrowly held: In 1989, the top 1 percent of families owned 39 percent of the wealth but received only (a still impressive) 16 percent of the income.

A particularly striking statistic in Wolff's book should put an end to the still-widespread tendency to discuss the growth of inequality in America by tracking the fortunes of the top 20 percent, or of college-educated workers. Between 1983 and 1989, while the wealth share of the top 20 percent of families rose substantially, the share of percentiles 80 to 99 actually fell. In other words, when we say that America's rich have gotten richer, by the "rich" we do not mean garden variety yuppies—we mean true plutocrats.

Many conservatives have probably stopped reading by now, or at least stopped being able to respond to this article with anything other than blind anger, but for those who are still with me let me make a crucial point about these statistics: *They say nothing about who, if anyone, is to blame.* To say that America was a far more unequal society in 1989 than it was in 1973 is a simple statement of fact, not an attack on Ronald Reagan. Think about the parable of the fishermen and the prospectors: The greater inequality of the latter society did not come about because it has worse leadership but because it lives in a different environment. And changes in the environment—in world markets, or in technology—might change a society of middle-class fishermen into a society with dismaying extremes of wealth and poverty, without it necessarily being the result of deliberate policies.

In fact, it's pretty certain that this is what has happened in the United States. Ronald Reagan did not single-handedly cause the incomes of the rich to soar and those of the poor to decline. He did cut taxes at the top and social programs at the bottom, but most of the growth in inequality took place in the marketplace, in the pretax incomes of families. (There is a wide range of opinion as to just what happened with the markets, though clearly technology and the changing international trade scene played big roles.) Furthermore, the upward trend in inequality began in the seventies under Nixon, Ford, and Carter and continues in the nineties under Clinton; similar trends, if not so dramatic, are visible in many other countries.

Yet income distribution is a politicized subject all the same. The reason is obvious: The extent of inequality is relevant for policymaking. In the fisherman society, for example, people might feel that only invalids, widows, and orphans deserve public support. In the vastly unequal prospecting world, however, it is easy to imagine a broad public demand that those who have been lucky enough to find gold be required to share a significant fraction of their winnings with those who have not. Indeed, it is hard to see how such a redistributionist program would *not* be popular—if the public understood just what was going on.

It is in the light of this possibility—that a redistributionist policy would have broad support if people understood the realities—that we should consider Armey's *The Freedom Revolution*. It is not, to say the least, a carefully written or argued book; it consists largely of standard conservative bromides, backed by a number of unsupported assertions. But despite the book's sloppiness, it is an important document, because of what it says about the majority leader's intellectual processes. Armey, a former economics professor, could have made the case that there is nothing that can or should be done about growing inequality. But instead he tries to claim, in essence, that nothing has happened—that we *really are* still a society of middle-class fishermen.

First, Armey denies that the eighties were a period in which the rich got richer and the poor got poorer. "The statisticians," he writes, "break our population into five income groups, called quintiles. During the eighties they gained in average real income as follows:

Lowest quintile—up 12.2 percent.
Second-lowest—up 10.1 percent.
Middle—up 10.7 percent.
Second-highest—up 11.6 percent.
Highest—up 18.8 percent."

The source for this data, not cited, is the Bureau of the Census's *Current Population Report*. This is helpful to know, because if you check Armey's facts you will find he is fibbing a bit. These figures are not income gains for all of the eighties, but only from 1983 to 1989. Immediately preceding that recovery, the economy experienced a savage recession, the worst since the Great Depression, that affected the poor much more severely than the rich. The first column of the table below gives the percentage changes for the slump years from 1979 to 1983.

Conservatives will say, "The recession was Carter's fault, while the recovery proved the success of Reagan's policies." But put politics aside for a moment and accept this simple fact: At the end of the 1983 to 1989 recovery, the bottom quintile was still worse off than it was in 1979, while the only really large gains over the decade went to the top quintile. If one takes the long view, as in the second column of the table (which measures from the business cycle peak in 1973), one sees an overwhelming picture of radically growing inequality. And one might correctly suspect even from these data that the pattern continued inside the top quintile, i.e., that the top 5 and the top 1 percent did better still.

When Armey (with his Ph.D. in economics) wrote this passage, he must have had the same table in front of him that I am looking at now. He must therefore have known that he was, strictly speaking, lying when he described his data as being what hap-

| Percentage Income Change by Income Bracket for the Periods 1979–1983 and 1973–1989. | | |
| --- | --- | --- |
| Income Bracket | 1979–1983 | 1973–1989 |
| Lowest quintile | -14.2 | -3.6 |
| Second lowest | -8.1 | 3.1 |
| Middle | -6.2 | 9.0 |
| Second highest | -2.9 | 14.8 |
| Highest | -1.4 | 26.0 |

pened during the "eighties," and could not have failed to notice that, even at the end of his carefully selected period, incomes were fare more unequal than they had been in the seventies. In other words, the passage is a deliberate attempt to mislead the reader.

It gets even better. Armey cites a study that shows that there is huge income mobility in America. The message here is simple: Don't worry that some people find gold and some don't—next year you may be the winner. He gives numbers saying that fewer than 15 percent of the "folks" who were in the bottom quintile in 1979 were still there in 1988. He then asserts that it was more likely that someone would move from the bottom quintile to the top than he would stay in place. Again, he doesn't cite the source, but these are familiar numbers. They come from a botched 1992 Bush administration study, a study that was immediately ridiculed and that its authors would just as soon forget.

This is why: The study tracked a number of people who had paid income taxes in each of the years from 1979 to 1988. Since only about half the working population actually paid taxes over the entire period, this meant that the study was already biased toward tracking the relatively successful. And these earners were then compared to *the population at large*. So the study showed that in 1979, 28 percent of this studied population was in the bottom 20 percent of the whole population; by 1988 that figure was only 7 percent.

This means, Armey asserts, that someone in the lowest quintile would be more likely to move to the highest than stay in place. Put kindly, it's a silly argument. For subjects of the study who moved from the bottom to the top, the typical age in 1979 was only 22. "This isn't your classic income mobility," Kevin Murphy of the University of Chicago remarked at the time. "This is the guy who works in the college bookstore and has a real job by the time he is in his early thirties."

In reality, moves from the bottom to the top quintile are

extremely rare; a typical estimate is that only about 3 percent of families who are in the bottom 20 percent in one year will be in the top 20 percent a decade later. About half will still be in the bottom quintile. And even those 3 percent that move aren't necessarily Horatio Alger stories. The top quintile includes everyone from a $60,000 a year regional manager to Warren Buffett.

Armey is no fool. He cannot be unaware that he is fudging his numbers. Possibly he regards a small fib as justifiable in the service of a higher truth. Or possibly he has managed to achieve a state of doublethink, in which the distinction between what is politically convenient to believe and the objective facts no longer exists. The end result is the same: His book is an effort to obscure the stark realities of growing inequality.

And that is no surprise. After all, the success of free-market conservatives in seizing the mantle of populism in America, despite the growing gap between the broad public and a small minority possessing astonishing wealth, is inherently vulnerable. It took a combination of brilliant political leadership on the right and an awesome mixture of political ineptitude, personal arrogance, and cultural elitism on the part of liberals to give Armey and their allies their current position of power. (I sometimes think that Renaissance Weekend killed the Clinton administration.)

But despite the triumph of 1994, there is always the risk that someone will point out that there are now quite a few men in America who each make more money every year than the entire House of Representatives, and that it is these men who will be the most conspicuous beneficiaries of the new majority's politics.

As far as Armey and his allies are concerned, the answer to this risk is simple: The public must not know how well the rich have done compared with the rest. If a new study points out just how much income and wealth have become concentrated, deploy the forces of the conservative media to attack the data with every spurious argument imaginable. There are always plenty of places to publish such attacks and people to write them because the rich are different from you and me: They have (a lot) more money. In particular, they own magazines and newspapers, and readily support think tanks staffed with people whose job, whatever its formal description, is to support the interests of their donors. As H. L. Mencken once pointed out, it is difficult to get a man to understand something when his income depends on his not understanding it.

The uneasy politics of free-market populism are also probably a major reason why the Republican majority in Congress seems determined to mount an assault on economic analysis in general— not only to eliminate the President's Council of Economic Advisers, but to eliminate all National Science Foundation funding for the field, and to slash the budget of the Bureau of Economic Analysis (which provides the basic data on national income).

The irony is that much of this research provides support for Republican free-market ideology. But the motivation for cutting the funding is easy enough to understand: If your doctrine depends on a view of the economy that is flatly contradicted by reality, then the fewer facts, the better.

Edward Wolff has written a good book, while Richard Armey has written a terrible one. The real message, however, comes from the contrast between them—between the mildly liberal economics professor who is disturbed by the trends in our society and would like to make a small effort to ameliorate them, and the tough-talking conservative who is determined to deny the reality of these trends and to smash anyone who reports on them. May the better man win.

# The Lost Fig Leaf: Why the Conservative Revolution Failed

"You now work from the first of January to May just to pay your taxes so that the party of government can satisfy its priorities with the sweat of your brow because they think that what you would do with your own money would be morally and practically less admirable than what they would do with it. . . . Somewhere, a grandmother couldn't afford to call her granddaughter, or a child went without a book, or a family couldn't afford that first home because there was just not enough money. . . . Why? Because some

Originally published in *Slate*, September 27, 1996.

genius in the Clinton administration took the money to fund yet another theory, yet another program, and yet another bureaucracy." The words are Bob Dole's (actually, they're Mark Helprin's, but Dole said them after accepting the Republican presidential nomination). They are the key to understanding why the Republican Revolution, which seemed so unstoppable at the beginning of 1995, ground to a halt within a year.

Dole's speech tried to put over, one more time, the fiction that the federal government takes away your hard-earned money and spends most of it on things that only social workers want. Supply-side economics, with its promise that tax cuts would pay for themselves, may have given conservatives the courage to be irresponsible. But what sold the public on conservatism was the images of vast armies of bureaucrats and of welfare queens driving Cadillacs. Conservatives were able to get away with such stories for one main reason: They could always blame their failure to slay Big Government on the Democrats who controlled Congress. Then they suddenly found themselves in control—and the fig leaf was gone. Some on the right attribute their troubles to mere tactical failures; if only Dole had been a better campaigner, if only Clinton hadn't shamelessly veered right, if only Gingrich hadn't thrown a tantrum on Air Force One, the conservative wave would have rolled on. And they insist that their defeats were only temporary setbacks. But the truth is that the political appeal of radical conservatism has always been based on a fundamentally untrue vision of what the federal government is and does.

To get an idea of the gap between conservative mythology and reality, let's look at the best book published in America. It's called *The Statistical Abstract of the United States*, and if more people would get into the habit of checking it, our politics would be utterly transformed. The *Statistical Abstract* makes it quite easy to get a realistic picture of where your tax dollar goes. For example, here is a list of ten major federal programs. The number after the colon indicates each program's percentage of fiscal 1994 spending:

Social Security: 21.6%

Defense: 18.9%

Interest on the debt: 13.7%

Medicare: 9.7%

Medicaid: 5.8%

Pensions for federal workers: 4.2%

Veterans' benefits: 2.6%

Transportation (mainly highways, air traffic, etc.): 2.6%

Unemployment insurance: 2.0%

Administration of justice (courts, law enforcement, etc.): 1.1%

There are three important things to say about this list. The first is that it encompasses the bulk of government spending—82.2 percent, to be precise. Anyone who proposes a radical downsizing of the federal government must mean to slash this list. The second is that with one possible exception, these are programs that the public likes—they are not at all what people object to when they rail against Big Government. We believe in honoring our debts. We like our strong military; indeed, most conservatives want it stronger. We like our highways. We want strong law enforcement. The only possibly unpopular item on the list is Medicaid, which is the only "poverty" program. But Medicaid is increasingly a program of aid not for the poor per se, but rather, for the old. More and more of it pays for nursing-home care—and many of those patients have middle-class children.

And that brings us to the third point: Aside from defense and interest payments, the U.S. government is now mainly—yes, mainly—in the business of taxing the young and giving money to the old. Look at that list, and consider how utterly shameless Dole was in imagining a grandmother who couldn't afford to call her granddaughter because she pays too much in taxes. That grandmother almost surely lives better than people of her age ever lived before, supported by Social Security checks that will greatly exceed the value of the contributions she and her husband paid into the system. And her children could easily have sent her the money for phone calls, except that their Medicare contributions had to cover her hip replacement.

There is a good case to be made that America's gerontocracy has gone too far, that we are too generous to our retirees, especially to those who could afford to do without some of those benefits. But that is not a case the right has ever made. An honest advocate of smaller government would campaign not against elitist bureaucrats but against nice middle-class retirees in their Florida condominiums. Somehow, that wasn't in Dole's speech.

It isn't as easy to summarize federal regulation as it is to summarize federal spending, but the basic point is similar: Most of what the government does is actually serving, not opposing, the public's will. Lots of people snicker at snail-darter jokes, but only a small minority wants to see a repeal of the clean-air or clean-water laws. And the voters are prepared to punish those politicians whom they suspect of belonging to that minority.

Of course, the federal government wastes a lot of money; so does the private sector (have you read "Dilbert" lately?). But the kind of oppressive government, run by meddling elitists, that Bob Dole tried to tell us about in San Diego exists only in the conservative imagination. And that is why Gingrich and Dole did not snatch defeat from the jaws of victory. Their reversal of fortune was preordained, because their doctrine could not withstand the responsibility that came with success.

# Gold Bug Variations:
# Understanding the
# Right-Wing Gilt Trip

The legend of King Midas has been generally misunderstood. Most people think the curse that turned everything the old miser touched into gold, leaving him unable to eat or drink, was a lesson in the perils of avarice. But Midas's true sin was his failure to understand monetary economics. What the gods were really telling him is that gold is just a metal. If it sometimes seems to be more, that is only because society has found it convenient to use gold as a medium of exchange—a bridge between other, truly

Originally published in *Slate*, November 22, 1996.

desirable, objects. There are other possible mediums of exchange, and it is silly to imagine that this pretty, but only moderately useful, substance has some irreplaceable significance.

But there are many people—nearly all of them ardent conservatives—who reject that lesson. While Jack Kemp, Steve Forbes, and *Wall Street Journal* editor Robert Bartley are best known for their promotion of supply-side economics, they are equally dedicated to the belief that the key to prosperity is a return to the gold standard, which John Maynard Keynes pronounced a "barbarous relic" more than sixty years ago. With any luck, these latter-day Midases will never lay a finger on actual monetary policy. Nonetheless, these are influential people—they are one of the factions now struggling for the Republican party's soul—and the passionate arguments they make for a gold standard are a useful window on how they think.

There *is* a case to be made for a return to the gold standard. It is not a very good case, and most sensible economists reject it, but the idea is not completely crazy. On the other hand, the ideas of our modern gold bugs *are* completely crazy. Their belief in gold is, it turns out, not pragmatic but mystical.

The current world monetary system assigns no special role to gold; indeed, the Federal Reserve is not obliged to tie the dollar to anything. It can print as much or as little money as it deems appropriate. There are powerful advantages to such an unconstrained system. Above all, the Fed is free to respond to actual or threatened recessions by pumping in money. To take only one example, that flexibility is the reason the stock market crash of 1987—which started out every bit as frightening as that of 1929—did not cause a slump in the real economy.

While a freely floating national money has advantages, however, it also has risks. For one thing, it can create uncertainties for international traders and investors. Over the past five years, the dollar has been worth as much as 120 yen and as little as 80. The costs of this volatility are hard to measure (partly because sophisticated financial markets allow businesses to hedge much of that risk), but they must be significant. Furthermore, a system that leaves monetary managers free to do good also leaves them free to be irresponsible—and, in some countries, they have been quick to take the opportunity. That is why countries with a history of runaway inflation, like Argentina, often come to the conclusion that monetary independence is a poisoned chalice. (Argentine law now requires that one peso be worth exactly one U.S. dollar, and that every peso in circulation be backed by a dollar in reserves.)

So, there is no obvious answer to the question of whether or not to tie a nation's currency to some external standard. By establishing a fixed rate of exchange between currencies—or even adopting a common currency—nations can eliminate the uncertainties of fluctuating exchange rates; and a country with a history of irresponsible policies may be able to gain credibility by association. (The Italian government wants to join a European Monetary Union largely because it hopes to refinance its massive debts at German interest rates.) On the other hand, what happens if two nations have joined their currencies, and one finds itself experiencing an inflationary boom while the other is in a deflationary recession? (This is exactly what happened to Europe in the early 1990s, when western Germany boomed while the rest of Europe slid into double-digit unemployment.) Then the monetary policy that is appropriate for one is exactly wrong for the other. These ambiguities explain why economists are divided over the wisdom of Europe's attempt to create a common currency. I personally think that it will lead, on average, to somewhat higher European unemployment rates; but many sensible economists disagree.

So where does gold enter the picture? While some modern nations have chosen, with reasonable justification, to renounce their monetary autonomy in favor of some external standard, the standard they choose these days is always the currency of another, presumably more responsible, nation. Argentina seeks salvation from the dollar; Italy from the deutsche mark. But the men and women who run the Fed, and even those who run the German Bundesbank, are mere mortals, who may yet succumb to the temptations of the printing press. Why not ensure monetary virtue by trusting not in the wisdom of men but in an objective standard? Why not emulate our great-grandfathers and tie our currencies to gold?

Very few economists think this would be a good idea. The argument against it is one of pragmatism, not principle. First, a gold standard would have all the disadvantages of any system of rigidly fixed exchange rates—and even economists who are enthusiastic about a common European currency generally think that fixing the European currency to the dollar or yen would be going too far. Second, and crucially, gold is not a stable standard when measured in terms of other goods and services. On the contrary, it is a commodity whose price is constantly buffeted by shifts in supply and demand that have nothing to do with the needs of the world economy—by changes, for example, in dentistry.

The United States abandoned its policy of stabilizing gold prices back in 1971. Since then the price of gold has increased roughly tenfold, while consumer prices have increased about 250 percent. If we had tried to keep the price of gold from rising, this would have required a massive decline in the prices of practically everything else—deflation on a scale not seen since the Depression. This doesn't sound like a particularly good idea.

So why are Jack Kemp, the *Wall Street Journal*, and so on so fixated on gold? I did not fully understand their position until I read a letter to, of all places, the left-leaning magazine *Mother Jones* from Jude Wanniski—one of the founders of supply-side economics and its reigning guru. Wanniski's main concern was to deny that the rich have gotten richer in recent decades; but the letter also contained the following noteworthy passage:

First let us get our accounting unit squared away. To measure anything in the floating paper dollar will get us nowhere. We must convert all wealth into the measure employed by mankind for 6,000 years, i.e., ounces of gold. On this measure, the Dow Jones industrial average of 6,000 today is only 60 percent of the DJIA of 30 years ago, when it hit 1,000. Back then, gold was $35 per ounce. Today it is $380-plus. This is another way of saying that in the last 30 years, the people who owned America have lost 40 percent of their wealth held in the form of equity. . . . If you owned no part of corporate America 30 years ago, because you were poor, you lost nothing. If you owned lots of it, you lost your shirt in the general inflation.

Never mind the question of whether the Dow Jones industrial average is the proper measure of how well the rich are doing. What is fascinating about this passage is that Wanniski regards gold as the appropriate measure of wealth, regardless of the quantity of other goods and services that it can buy. Since the dollar was delinked from gold in 1971, the Dow has risen about 700 percent, while the prices of the goods we ordinarily associate with the pursuit of happiness—food, houses, clothes, cars, servants—have gone up only about 250 percent. In terms of the ability to buy almost anything except gold, the purchasing power of the rich has soared; but Wanniski insists that this is irrelevant, because gold, and only gold, is the true standard of value. Wanniski, in other words, has committed the sin of King Midas: He has forgotten that gold is only a metal, and that its value comes only from the truly useful goods for which it can be exchanged.

I wonder whether the gods check out my columns. If so, they know what to do.

*Part 3*

# Globalization and Globaloney

*T*he useful term "globaloney" was coined by none other than Claire Booth Luce. What she had in mind was gaseous talk about geopolitics, but the term applies equally well to the way many modern pundits ascribe everything that happens in the world to the vaguely defined impacts of the global economy. Globalization is, of course, a real phenomenon: International trade and investment have consistently grown faster than the world economy as a whole, so that national economies have steadily become more interdependent. But both the extent of that interdependence and its impacts are usually exaggerated. And among intellectuals, at least, there is a strong tendency to demonize the whole phenomenon—to blame it for all the evils in the world, and to deny that growing trade and investment could possibly be doing anybody except fat-cat capitalists any good.

The first essay here, "We Are Not the World," is an attempt at a corrective—an effort to explain that America, at least, is nowhere near to being a mere pawn of global economic forces. When the original version of the piece was published, I was surprised at the vehemence of some of the responses—and also surprised that so much of the vitriol was focused not on the main argument, but on a side remark I had made, to the effect that many poor people in the Third World had benefited from globalization. I guess I had thought that was obvious—but it turned out to demand a fuller discussion, which I tried to provide in the next essay, "In Praise of Cheap Labor."

Finally, "The East Is in the Red" deals with a view that has rapidly achieved prominence among some pundits and politicians: the view that the rise of newly industrializing economies will lead to a global glut, that these economies—China in particular—will produce but not consume, export but not import. In this essay I tried to use the reunification of Hong Kong with China as an occasion to take this view on, trying to show that it represents a misunderstanding of both the facts and the theory of the case— and along the way to give readers a quick, painless lesson in the economics of trade balances.

# *We Are Not the World*

It is a truth universally acknowledged that the growing international mobility of goods, capital, and technology has completely changed the economic game. Nations, conventional wisdom tells us, no longer have the power to control their own destinies; governments are at the mercy of international markets.

Some celebrate this development, saying that both rich and poor nations benefit. At the same time, a growing number of jour-

Originally published in *New York Times*, February 13, 1997. Copyright © 1997 by the New York Times Co. Reprinted by permission.

nalists, union leaders, politicians of both parties, and even businessmen deplore it, blaming globalization for instability, unemployment, and declining wages.

But both sides have it wrong. They take the omnipotence of global markets for granted—not realizing that reports of the death of national autonomy are greatly exaggerated.

A certain fascination with the march of globalization is understandable. For half a century, world trade has grown faster than world output, and international capital now moves more quickly than ever before. The rapidly expanding exports of newly industrializing economies have put pressure on less-skilled workers in advanced countries even as they offer unprecedented opportunities to tens of millions in the Third World. (As discussed in the next essay, the wages of those workers are shockingly low but nonetheless represent a vast improvement on their previous, less visible rural poverty.)

But while global economic integration is increasing, its growth has been far outpaced by that of "global economy" rhetoric. William Greider's recent book *One World, Ready or Not* is a jeremiad about the evils of unfettered economic globalism. Politicians like Pat Buchanan and Ross Perot have made careers out of assailing open markets. Even the financier George Soros warns, in the *Atlantic Monthly*, that global capitalism is now a greater threat than totalitarianism to "open society."

Such oratory has become so pervasive that many observers seem determined to blame global markets for a host of economic and social ills in their countries, even when the facts point unmistakably to mainly domestic—and usually political—causes.

For example, critics of globalization often cite France, whose government has taken no serious action to reduce its double-digit unemployment rate, as the perfect example of how states have become powerless in the face of impersonal world markets. France cannot act, according to a recent *New York Times* article, because of the demands of "European economic integration—itself partly a response to the competitive demands of the global marketplace."

French policy is indeed paralyzed—not, however, by impersonal market forces but by the determination of its prestige-conscious politicians not to let the franc decline against the German mark. Britain, which has been willing to let the pound sink relative to the mark, has steadily reduced its unemployment rate with no visible adverse consequences. The cause of France's paralysis, in other words, is political rather than economic. True, the country must meet the conditions laid down by the Maastricht Treaty of 1991, which is supposed to lead to a unified European currency. But creating this currency is more a political than an economic project. Its main purpose is to serve as a symbol of European unity, and many economists think that the costs of the common currency will exceed its benefits. It would actually be more accurate to say that French politics has battered markets rather than the other way around.

And what about the United States, where the continuing power of the government—or at any rate that of the Federal Reserve—to push the economy around can hardly be questioned? Critics of the global economy invariably reply that America may be creating lots of jobs but that they are tenuous because of the prevalence of downsizing, which is a reaction to international competition (a line of reasoning that also provides a good excuse for companies undertaking layoffs).

Come again? Early in 1996, *Newsweek* ran a story titled "The Hit Men," about executives responsible for massive layoffs. The chief executives of AT&T, Nynex, Sears, Philip Morris, and Delta Air Lines were high on the list. Of course, international competition plays a role in some downsizings, but as *Newsweek*'s list makes clear, it is hardly the most important cause of the phenomenon. To my knowledge there are no Japanese keiretsu competing to carry my long-distance calls or South Korean conglomerates offering me local phone service. Nor have many Americans started buying their home appliances at Mexican stores or smoking French cigarettes. I cannot fly Cathay Pacific from Boston to New York.

What explains this propensity to overstate the importance of global markets? In part, it sounds sophisticated. Pontificating about globalization is an easy way to get attention at events like the World Economic Forum in Davos, Switzerland, and Renaissance Weekends in Hilton Head, S.C.

But there is also a deeper cause—an odd sort of tacit agreement between the Left and the Right to pretend that exotic global forces are at work even when the real action is prosaically domestic.

Many on the Left dislike the global marketplace because it epitomizes what they dislike about markets in general: the fact that nobody is in charge. The truth is that the invisible hand rules most domestic markets, too, a reality that most Americans seem to accept as a fact of life. But those who would like to see us revert to a more managed society in all ways hope that popular unease over the economic influence of people who live in far-off places and have funny-sounding names can be used as the thin end of an ideological wedge. Meanwhile, many on the Right use the rhetoric of globalization to argue that business can no longer be expected to meet any social obligations. For example, it has become standard for opponents of environmental regulations to raise the banner of "competitiveness" and to warn that anything that raises costs for American businesses will price our goods out of world markets.

But even if the global economy matters less than the sweeping assertions would have us believe, does this "globaloney," as the cognoscenti call it, do any real harm? Yes, in part because the public, misguided into believing that international trade is the source of all our problems, might turn protectionist—undermining the real good that globalization has done for most people here and abroad. But the overheated oratory poses a more subtle risk. It encourages fatalism, a sense that we cannot come to grips with our problems because they are bigger than we are. Such fatalism is already well advanced in Western Europe, where the public speaks vaguely of the "economic horror" inflicted by world markets instead of turning a critical eye on the domestic leaders whose policies have failed.

None of the important constraints on American economic and social policy come from abroad. We have the resources to take far better care of our poor and unlucky than we do; if our policies have become increasingly mean-spirited, that is a political choice, not something imposed on us by anonymous forces. We cannot evade responsibility for our actions by claiming that global markets made us do it.

# In Praise of Cheap Labor: Bad Jobs at Bad Wages Are Better than No Jobs at All

For many years a huge Manila garbage dump known as Smokey Mountain was a favorite media symbol of Third World poverty. Several thousand men, women, and children lived on that dump—enduring the stench, the flies, and the toxic waste in order to make a living combing the garbage for scrap metal and other recyclables. And they lived there voluntarily, because the ten dollars or so a squatter family could clear in a day was better than the alternatives.

The squatters are gone now, forcibly removed by Philippine

Originally published in *Slate*, March 20, 1997.

police in 1996 as a cosmetic move in advance of a Pacific Rim summit. But I found myself thinking about Smokey Mountain recently, after reading my latest batch of hate mail.

The occasion was an op-ed piece I had written for the *New York Times* ("We Are Not the World"), in which I had pointed out that while wages and working conditions in the new export industries of the Third World are appalling, they are a big improvement over the "previous, less visible rural poverty." I guess I should have expected that this comment would generate letters along the lines of, "Well, if you lose your comfortable position as an American professor you can always find another job—as long as you are twelve years old and willing to work for two dollars a day."

Such moral outrage is common among the opponents of globalization—of the transfer of technology and capital from high-wage to low-wage countries and the resulting growth of labor-intensive Third World exports. These critics take it as a given that anyone with a good word for this process is naive or corrupt and, in either case, a de facto agent of global capital in its oppression of workers here and abroad.

But matters are not that simple, and the moral lines are not that clear. In fact, let me make a counter-accusation: The lofty moral tone of the opponents of globalization is possible only because they have chosen not to think their position through. While fat-cat capitalists might benefit from globalization, the biggest beneficiaries are, yes, Third World workers.

After all, global poverty is not something recently invented for the benefit of multinational corporations. Let's turn the clock back to the Third World as it was only two decades ago (and still is, in many countries). In those days, although the rapid economic growth of a handful of small Asian nations had started to attract attention, developing countries like Indonesia or Bangladesh were still mainly what they had always been: exporters of raw materials, importers of manufactures. Inefficient manufacturing sectors served their domestic markets, sheltered behind import quotas, but generated few jobs. Meanwhile, population pressure pushed desperate peasants into cultivating ever more marginal land or seeking a livelihood in any way possible—such as homesteading on a mountain of garbage.

Given this lack of other opportunities, you could hire workers in Jakarta or Manila for a pittance. But in the mid-seventies, cheap labor was not enough to allow a developing country to compete in world markets for manufactured goods. The entrenched advantages of advanced nations—their infrastructure and technical know-how, the vastly larger size of their markets and their proximity to suppliers of key components, their political stability and the subtle-but-crucial social adaptations that are necessary to operate an efficient economy—seemed to outweigh even a tenfold or twentyfold disparity in wage rates.

And then something changed. Some combination of factors that we still don't fully understand—lower tariff barriers, improved telecommunications, cheaper air transport—reduced the disadvantages of producing in developing countries. (Other things being the same, it is still better to produce in the First World—stories of companies that moved production to Mexico or East Asia, then moved back after experiencing the disadvantages of the Third World environment, are common.) In a substantial number of industries, low wages allowed developing countries to break into world markets. And so countries that had previously made a living selling jute or coffee started producing shirts and sneakers instead.

Workers in those shirt and sneaker factories are, inevitably, paid very little and are expected to endure terrible working conditions. I say "inevitably" because their employers are not in business for their (or their workers') health; they pay as little as possible, and that minimum is determined by the other opportunities available to workers. And these are still extremely poor countries, where living on a garbage heap is attractive compared with the alternatives.

And yet, wherever the new export industries have grown, there has been measurable improvement in the lives of ordinary people. Partly this is because a growing industry must offer a somewhat higher wage than workers could get elsewhere in order to get them to move. More importantly, however, the growth of manufacturing—and of the penumbra of other jobs that the new export sector creates—has a ripple effect throughout the economy. The pressure on the land becomes less intense, so rural wages rise; the pool of unemployed urban dwellers always anxious for work shrinks, so factories start to compete with each other for workers, and urban wages also begin to rise. Where the process has gone on long enough—say, in South Korea or Taiwan—average wages start to approach what an American teenager can earn at McDonald's. And eventually people are no longer eager to live on garbage dumps. (Smokey Mountain persisted because the Philippines, until recently, did not share in the export-led growth of its neighbors. Jobs that pay better than scavenging are still few and far between.)

The benefits of export-led economic growth to the mass of people in the newly industrializing economies are not a matter of conjecture. A country like Indonesia is still so poor that progress can be measured in terms of how much the average person gets to eat; since 1970, per capita intake has risen from less than 2,100 to more than 2,800 calories a day. A shocking one-third of young children are still malnourished—but in 1975, the fraction was more than half. Similar improvements can be seen throughout the Pacific Rim, and even in places like Bangladesh. These improvements have not taken place because well-meaning people in the West have done anything to help—foreign aid, never large, has lately shrunk to virtually nothing. Nor is it the result of the benign policies of national governments, which are as callous and corrupt as ever. It is the indirect and unintended result of the actions of soulless multinationals and rapacious local entrepreneurs, whose only concern was to take advantage of the profit opportunities offered by cheap labor. It is not an edifying spectacle; but no matter how base the motives of those involved, the result has been to move hundreds of millions of people from abject poverty to something still awful but nonetheless significantly better.

Why, then, the outrage of my correspondents? Why does the image of an Indonesian sewing sneakers for sixty cents an hour evoke so much more feeling than the image of another Indonesian earning the equivalent of thirty cents an hour trying to feed his family on a tiny plot of land—or of a Filipino scavenging on a garbage heap?

The main answer, I think, is a sort of fastidiousness. Unlike the starving subsistence farmer, the women and children in the sneaker factory are working at slave wages *for our benefit*—and this makes us feel unclean. And so there are self-righteous demands for international labor standards: We should not, the opponents of globalization insist, be willing to buy those sneakers and shirts unless the people who make them receive decent wages and work under decent conditions.

This sounds only fair—but is it? Let's think through the consequences.

First of all, even if we could assure the workers in Third World export industries of higher wages and better working conditions, this would do nothing for the peasants, day laborers, scavengers, and so on who make up the bulk of these countries' populations. At best, forcing developing countries to adhere to our labor standards would create a privileged labor aristocracy, leaving the poor majority no better off.

And it might not even do that. The advantages of established First World industries are still formidable. The only reason developing countries have been able to compete with those industries is their ability to offer employers cheap labor. Deny them that ability, and you might well deny them the prospect of continuing industrial growth, even reverse the growth that has been achieved. And since export-oriented growth, for all its injustice, has been a huge boon for the workers in those nations, anything that curtails that growth is very much against their interests. A policy of good jobs in principle, but no jobs in practice, might assuage our consciences, but it is no favor to its alleged beneficiaries.

You may say that the wretched of the earth should not be forced to serve as hewers of wood, drawers of water, and sewers of sneakers for the affluent. But what is the alternative? Should they be helped with foreign aid? Maybe—although the historical record of regions like southern Italy suggests that such aid has a tendency to promote perpetual dependence. Anyway, there isn't the slightest prospect of significant aid materializing. Should their own governments provide more social justice? Of course—but they won't, or at least not because we tell them to. And as long as you have no realistic alternative to industrialization based on low wages, to oppose it means that you are willing to deny desperately poor people the best chance they have of progress for the sake of what amounts to an aesthetic standard—that is, the fact that you don't like the idea of workers being paid a pittance to supply rich Westerners with fashion items.

In short, my correspondents are not entitled to their self-righteousness. They have not thought the matter through. And when the hopes of hundreds of millions are at stake, thinking things through is not just good intellectual practice. It is a moral duty.

## A Note on Globalization

My favorite concrete example of the driving forces behind globalization is the recent and rapid rise of Zimbabwe's vegetable exports. In recent years, truck farmers near Harare have got into the business of supplying fresh vegetables to London markets. The vegetables are picked and trucked immediately to the airport, flown through the night to Heathrow, and are there on the shelf in Tesco the next morning.

This export business depends on at least three things. First, it depends on cheap air transport—the beat-up old Boeings that have become the tramp steamers of modern commerce. Second, it depends on modern telecommunications—the vegetables are delivered to order, which means that messages must be sent to the farmers in a way that used to be possible only in advanced countries with good phone systems. Finally, of course, the trade depends on an open British market. It could not happen if import quotas or high tariffs prevented the sales.

Now how do you feel about all of this? Here are some facts: The vegetables are produced using "appropriate technology"—that is, they are hand-grown and handpicked, using labor-intensive methods with relatively little machinery. As a result, the truck farms create quite a few jobs in an economy that desperately needs them. They are nonetheless cost-competitive because the workers are paid low wages, which they are happy to get given the lack of other opportunities. And, oh yes, the workers are black—and not only are their British customers white, but the farmers who employ them are white colonial settlers who have chosen to stay on under the new regime.

# The East Is in the Red: A Balanced View of China's Trade

Want an easy way to eliminate the U.S. trade deficit? Just declare New York City a separate "entity," with its own balance-of-payments statistics. I can almost guarantee you that the trade deficit of the rest of the country—call it "mainland America"—will disappear.

After all, if New York's numbers were counted separately, we would no longer treat goods imported into New York as debit items in the U.S. balance of payments. Furthermore, all of the

Originally published in *Slate*, July 17, 1997.

goods that mainland America ships to New York City would be considered U.S. exports. True, the goods that New York ships to the rest of the world would be struck off the export tally, while the goods the city ships to the rest of the United States would henceforth count as U.S. imports. But these would be minor adjustments: New York City is basically not in the business of producing physical objects. So we can be sure that the city runs a huge trade deficit—probably bigger than that of the United States as a whole, which is why splitting it off from the rest of the country would give the mainland a surplus.

Of course, most if not all of New York's deficit in *goods* trade is made up for by exports (to mainland America and the world at large) of intangibles such as financial services and tickets to see *Cats;* and the city also has a disproportionate number of wealthy residents, who receive lots of income from the property they own elsewhere. It would not be surprising to find that the city actually runs a surplus on its "current account," a measure that includes trade in services and investment income as well as the merchandise trade balance. But if it's the trade deficit you worry about, splitting New York off from mainland America will take care of the problem. Nothing real would have changed, but maybe it would make some people feel better.

What inspires this idea is China's assumption of political control over Hong Kong, which removes the last faint excuse for treating China and Hong Kong as separate economies—and therefore offers a way to make some of the same people feel better about another trade issue, the supposed threat posed by China's trade surplus. In recent years, China-sans-Hong Kong—what we used to call "mainland China"—has been running large and growing surpluses in its merchandise trade (although its balance on current account has fluctuated around zero). But China-plus-Hong Kong does not run big trade surpluses. In the year ending in April 1997, China ran a trade surplus of almost $24 billion—but Hong

Kong, as one would expect for a mainly service-producing city-state, ran an offsetting deficit of $19 billion, reducing the total to a fairly unimpressive $4.6 billion. China's trade surpluses, in other words, are largely a statistical illusion produced by the fact that so much of the management and ownership of the country's industry is located on the other side of an essentially arbitrary line.

Pointing this out doesn't change anything real, but perhaps it may help calm some of the fears being fostered by underemployed Japan-bashers who, like old cold warriors, have lately gone searching for new enemies.

Professional trade alarmist Alan Tonelson gave a particularly clear statement of the new fears in his *New York Times* review of *The Big Ten: The Big Emerging Markets and How They Will Change Our Lives,* a book by former Commerce Undersecretary Jeffrey Garten. (The review caught my eye because some of it matched word for word a speech by House Minority Leader and presidential hopeful Richard Gephardt.) After praising Garten for taking seriously the possibility that "the growing ability of the 10 to produce sophisticated goods and services at rock-bottom prices could drag down the standard of living of even affluent, well-educated Americans," Tonelson chided him for imagining that developing countries, China included, would provide important new markets for advanced-country exports: "[C]onsumer markets in these emerging countries are likely to stay small for decades . . . if they don't keep wages and purchasing power low, they will have trouble attracting the foreign investment they require, both to service debt and to finance growth."

I am always grateful when influential pundits make such statements, especially in prominent places, for in so doing they protect us from the ever-present temptation to take people seriously simply because they are influential, to imagine that widely held views must actually make at least some sense.

Tonelson's claim is that as emerging economies grow—that is, produce and sell greatly increased quantities of goods and services—their spending will not grow by a comparable amount; equivalently, he is claiming that they will run massive trade surpluses. But when a country grows, its total income must, by definition, rise one-for-one with the value of its production. Maybe you don't think that income will get paid out in higher wages, but it has to show up *somewhere*. And why should we imagine that people in emerging countries, unlike people in advanced nations, cannot find things to spend their money on?

In fact, one might well expect that emerging economies would typically run trade (or at least current account) deficits. After all, such countries will presumably attract inflows of foreign investment, allowing them to invest more than they save—which is to say, spend more than they earn. To put it another way, a country that attracts enough foreign investment "both to service debt and to finance growth" must, by definition, buy more goods and services than it sells—that is, run a trade deficit. The point, again, is that the money has to show up *somewhere*.

How can a country run a trade deficit when it has the huge cost advantage that comes from combining First World productivity with Third World wages? The answer is that the premise must be wrong: When productivity in emerging economies rises, so must wages—that is, the supposed situation in which these countries are able to "produce sophisticated goods and services at rock-bottom prices" never materializes.

I am sure that, despite its logic, my position sounds unrealistic to many readers. After all, in reality Third World countries *do* run massive trade surpluses, and their wages *don't* rise with productivity—right?

Well, let's do some abstruse statistical research—by, say, buying a copy of the *Economist* and opening it to the last page, which each week conveniently offers tables summarizing economic data for a number of emerging economies. We immediately learn something interesting: Of Garten's Big Ten, six run trade deficits (as does the group as a whole); nine run current account deficits. Of the twenty-five economies listed, seventeen run trade deficits and twenty run current account deficits. Wage numbers are a little harder to come by, but the U.S. Bureau of Labor Statistics makes such data available on its Foreign Labor Statistics Web site. There we find that in 1975, workers in Taiwan and South Korea received only 6 percent as much per hour as their counterparts in the United States; by 1995, the numbers were 34 percent and 43 percent, respectively.

Surprise! The facts fit the Panglossian economist's vision quite nicely: Emerging economies do typically run trade deficits, wages do rise with productivity, and actual experience offers no support at all for grimmer visions.

But those grim visions persist nonetheless. For smart people like Tonelson (or Gephardt), this cannot be a matter of simple ignorance: It must involve ignorance with intent. After all, it must require real effort for a full-time trade commentator, who not only writes frequently about the Third World threat but also decorates his writings with many statistics, not to notice that most of those countries run trade deficits rather than surpluses, or that wages have in fact increased dramatically in countries that used to have cheap labor. It is, I imagine, equally difficult to pursue such a career without ever becoming aware of the arithmetical necessity that countries attracting big inflows of capital must run trade deficits.

But perhaps the uncanny ability not to notice these things is acquired by focusing mainly on China, which does appear to run a huge trade surplus even while attracting lots of foreign capital. Most of that trade surplus, as we've seen, is a statistical illusion. But it is still, at first sight, hard to understand how China can attract so much foreign investment without running a large current account deficit. Where does the money go?

A useful clue comes if we look again at the last page of the *Economist* and ask which country runs the biggest trade surplus of all. And the answer is . . . *Russia*. Obviously this isn't because Russia's economy is super-competitive. What that trade surplus actually reflects is Russia's sorry state, in which nervous businessmen and corrupt officials siphon off a large fraction of the country's foreign exchange earnings, parking it in safe havens abroad rather than making it available to pay for imports.

China, if you think about it, suffers from a milder form of the same ailment. The reason those inflows of foreign capital don't finance a trade deficit is that they are offset by outflows of domestic capital. In particular, huge sums are being invested abroad to establish overseas nest eggs for honest Hong Kong businessmen just in case Hong Kong ends up looking like the rest of China, and no doubt to establish similar nest eggs for corrupt Chinese officials just in case the rest of China ends up looking like Hong Kong. To the extent that China does run a trade surplus, in other words, that surplus is a sign of weakness rather than strength.

None of this should be taken as an apology for China's thoroughly nasty government. I fear the worst in Hong Kong, and worry as much as anyone about the effects of growing Chinese power on Asia's political and military stability. One thing I don't worry about, however, is China's trade surplus. Neither should you.

## Note to "The East Is in the Red"

Most China-bashing in this country has concentrated not on China-sans-Hong Kong's overall trade surplus, but on its apparently even larger bilateral surplus in trade with the United States. I say "apparently" because there is considerable dispute about the numbers. The problem is—not surprisingly—the difficulty of disentangling the Chinese and Hong Kong economies. Many U.S. exports to China go through Hong Kong, and most experts agree that as a result U.S. statistics overstate exports to Hong Kong and understate those to China. That $50 billion number you often hear is surely too large; $30 billion is more like it. Of course, even if this weren't true it would be as silly to focus on the China–United States balance alone as to evaluate U.S. trade with, say, Canada while ignoring the imports and exports of New York City.

What a number of analysts have pointed out in particular is that the rise of U.S. imports from China has largely reflected a relocation of production that formerly took place in Hong Kong and Taiwan—and that while America's deficit vis-à-vis China has surged, its deficits vis-à-vis the other two have plunged. The overall trade deficit with Greater China (all three) has increased over time, but not nearly as much as the simple bilateral balance.

But I would argue for a deeper way of looking at the emergence of a large United States–China bilateral imbalance. That imbalance does indeed reflect an asymmetry between open markets in the United States and closed markets somewhere else—but that somewhere else is not China. Rather, the problem lies in other advanced countries, notably Japan.

Bear in mind that overall trade balances are determined by the balance between savings and investment; to a first approximation they have nothing to do with trade policies. Now imagine that a new producer emerges, eager to export labor-intensive products, prepared to import a roughly equal value of skill- or capital-intensive products. But while some countries (like the United States) have markets that are pretty open to that producer's exports, others (like Japan or France) have tacit barriers making it difficult for the emerging economy to sell there. What will happen, clearly, is that the new producer will sell a large fraction of its exports to the more open market, while it will not buy as large a fraction of its imports from that country. That is why China ends up running a large bilateral surplus with the United States.

Remember, however, that overall trade balances are tied down by the savings-investment balance. So the open-market United States will make up for its new deficit vis-à-vis China by running larger surpluses or smaller deficits with other countries (with the mechanism for this shift probably being some weakening of the dollar against other advanced-country currencies). Meanwhile, China will offset its trade surplus vis-à-vis the United States by running deficits vis-à-vis other countries. In effect, the world economy engages in a game of scissors-paper-stone: China takes markets previously held by America, America takes markets from other advanced countries, and these countries make up the difference by selling to China. It may seem that America is bearing an excessive burden, being required to accept the lion's (dragon's?) share of Chinese exports without gaining a comparable share of the Chinese market. But this is the wrong way to look at it; in fact, on most counts the United States gets the better deal.

First of all, to suggest that the United States does worse than other countries, because it allows in imports while they don't, brings to mind the classic comment of the nineteenth-century economist Frédéric Bastiat: It's like saying that we should block up our harbors because other nations have rocky coasts. By accepting labor-intensive imports from China and producing other things instead, the United States is taking advantage of the opportunity to stop doing things it does relatively badly and concentrate on doing things it does relatively well. Meanwhile, other advanced countries are denying themselves that opportunity: The kinds of goods they will start selling to China will be pretty similar to the goods they stop selling to or start buying from the United States.

Moreover, to the extent that you think some industries are more important than others—for example, because they yield technological spillovers—the jobs the United States gains by rolling back Japanese and European market shares in computers or semiconductors are surely more likely to produce those benefits than the jobs we give up by allowing in Chinese shirts and footwear.

The downside—which is significant—is that precisely because our more open markets lead us to gain high-wage jobs but lose low-wage employment, our disproportionate role as a market for Chinese exports may exacerbate the problem of growing income inequality.

The important thing to bear in mind is that the bilateral imbalance between the United States and China does not mean that the Chinese are taking advantage of our naiveté. (Which is not to say that they wouldn't if they could.) It is mainly the result of the restrictions third parties place on China's exports, not the restrictions China places on ours. And we are not being taken advantage of: In fact, the imbalance is actually a sign that America is taking advantage of opportunities that other advanced countries are passing up.

## Part 4

# Delusions of Growth

*F*ew subjects in economics are as contentious as the business cycle—those fluctuations of output and unemployment around the long-run upward trend. A generation ago economists were all pretty much agreed on what caused business cycles. Then, partly as a result of "stagflation"—the unexpected and unpleasant combination of inflation and unemployment that emerged in the 1970s—but mainly as a result of differences in methodological tastes, economists studying the business cycle divided into rival factions. Some argued for an updated version of the old, mainly Keynesian approach; others wanted to reject it entirely. The great business cycle theory wars did huge damage to the prestige of economics as a profession; they also created a sense that nobody knew anything, which opened the door for various crank doctrines—most notably supply-side economics.

Don't tell anybody, but those wars are basically over. (Princeton's Alan Blinder calls this the "clean little secret of macroeconomics.") While the factions still tend to use different language, their actual views have converged—to something not very different from the consensus view of a generation ago. But the damage has proved hard to repair: many people still think that economics has nothing useful to say about the business cycle, and crank doctrines continue to flourish.

The crank doctrine *du jour* is something widely known as the "New Paradigm"; it amounts to the assertion that new forces such as globalization and technological change have cancelled all the old rules, that old speed limits on growth have been repealed, perhaps that the business cycle itself has been abolished. There are many things wrong with that story line, among them the question of whether globalization and technology are really proceeding as dramatically as its adherents claim. "We Are Not the World" already described my doubts about globalization; the first essay here describes some similar doubts about technology.

More important, however, the New Paradigm seems to involve confusion about the difference between the business cycle and long-term growth, coupled with a misunderstanding of the things that monetary policy can and cannot do. I try to explain those distinctions in the second essay, "Four Percent Follies."

To be skeptical about the prospects for rapid growth is, it turns out, to run the risk of being identified with another, equally misguided camp: that which believes that controlling inflation is the only priority of policy, that nothing can be done to fight recession and unemployment. This belief, especially acute among central bankers, is arguably imposing huge, gratuitous economic pain in much of the world; the third piece here, "A Good Word for Inflation," focuses mainly on Europe and makes the case against a single-minded emphasis on price stability, while the fourth essay argues that monetary passivity accounts for much (not all) of Japan's economic malaise.

Finally, in "Seeking the Rule of the Waves," I made use of a book review assignment to say some things I always wanted to say about economics, history, and the reasons why the business cycle is surely nowhere near dead.

# Technology's Wonders: Not So Wondrous

Lately many business leaders and thinkers have become preoccupied with something called the Information Technology Paradox. It goes like this: We live in an age of unprecedented technological progress, which is making everyone far more efficient than before. Yet where is the payoff? The standard of living of ordinary Americans doesn't seem to be soaring; if anything, many people are finding it harder, not easier, to make ends meet. If we're so smart, why aren't we richer?

Originally published in *USA Today*, December 12, 1996.

A lot of ingenious things have been said about the reasons for the paradox, but there is one explanation that hardly anyone dares mention: Maybe the wonders of technology we keep hearing about aren't really all that wondrous.

To get an idea of what I mean, think about *2001*. No, not the year—the movie *2001: A Space Odyssey*, which came out in 1968. Most readers must have seen it. The middle part of the movie offered what was supposed to be a realistic picture of life thirty-three years in the movie's future, but barely four years from now. In that world there were regularly scheduled commercial flights to space stations with Sheraton-style lobbies, and computers smart enough to go on a postal worker–style rampage when they felt unappreciated. But airlines aren't offering orbital vacations to their frequent flyers; Shannon Lucid could not call room service; and my computer's idea of murderous revenge is to tell me "An error has occurred in your application. Terminate/Ignore?" If 2001 is actually going to look anything like *2001*, technology had better get a move on.

The point is that if you measure the progress of technology not by Mips and bytes but by how it affects people's lives and their ability to get useful work done, you realize that the last thirty years have been a time not of unexpected achievement but of persistent disappointment.

Surely, for example, the startling thing about computers is not how fast and small they have become but how stupid they remain. Back in 1958 the pioneer computer scientist Herbert Simon confidently predicted that a computer would be the world's chess champion by 1970; this makes the eventual victory of IBM's Deep Blue over Gary Kasparov a bit of a letdown. And building a computer that plays high-level chess turns out to be an easy problem—nowhere near as hard as, say, designing a robot that can vacuum your living room, an achievement that is still probably many decades away.

Originally published in *CSI Tech*, December 22, 1998.

Even where computers have become ubiquitous—such as in the modern office—it is very questionable how much they actually raise productivity. Recently many companies have begun to realize that when they equip their office workers with computers they also impose huge hidden costs on themselves—because a computer requires technical support, frequent purchases of new software, repeated retraining of employees, and so on. That $2,000 computer on your employee's desk may well impose $8,000 a year in such hidden costs—and that's even if the worker does not spend a significant part of the work day playing Tetris or surfing the Net.

And what about technologies that *don't* involve manipulating digital information—for example, the technology of daily life? Think, for example, about how a typical middle-class family lives today compared with forty years ago—and compare those changes with the progress that took place over the previous forty years.

I happen to be an expert on some of those changes, because I live in a house with a late-fifties-vintage kitchen, never remodelled. The non-self-defrosting refrigerator and the gas range with its open pilot lights are pretty depressing (anyone know a good contractor?)—but when all is said and done it is still a pretty functional kitchen. The 1957 owners didn't have a microwave, and we have gone from black and white broadcasts of Sid Caesar to off-color humor on The Comedy Channel, but basically they lived pretty much the way we do. Now turn the clock back another forty years, to 1917—and you are in a world in which a horse-drawn wagon delivered blocks of ice to your icebox, a world not only without TV but without mass media of any kind (regularly scheduled radio entertainment began only in 1920). And of course back in 1917 nearly half of Americans still lived on farms, most without electricity and many without running water. By any reasonable standard, the change in how America lived between 1917 and 1957 was immensely greater than the change between 1957 and the present.

In short, the idea that we are living in an age of dramatic technological progress is mainly hype; the reality is that we live in a time when the fundamental things are actually not changing very rapidly at all.

Now I am not saying that this is anyone's fault. If Bill Gates turns out to be no Henry Ford, that is no reflection on his abilities. Really productive ideas, like internal combustion and the assembly line, are hard to find. It is no tragedy if we have to make do with second-rate inventions like the personal computer until the next Model T comes along. But the techno-hype that surrounds us has some real costs. It causes businesses to waste money; it causes politicians to seek high-tech fixes (give every child a laptop!) when they should be getting back to the basics (teach every child to read). The slightly depressing truth is that technology has been letting us down lately. Let's face up to that truth, and get on with our lives.

# Four Percent Follies

Recently a lot of influential people have been berating Alan Greenspan and his colleagues at the Federal Reserve for not allowing the economy to grow faster. The most prominent of these critics has probably been Felix Rohatyn, who was proposed though never formally nominated to become the vice-chairman of the Fed. It's important to note that Rohatyn is not arguing for a modest change in policy, a view that many economists share. What he is arguing for is a massive monetary expansion: instead of the 2 to

A talk given to the Economic Club of Washington, April 1996.

2.5 percent growth the Fed seems to be targeting, it should aim for no less than 3.5 or 4 percent over the next decade. In fact, let me refer to Rohatyn and allies for short as the "four-percenters."

This debate over Fed policy is obviously a crucial issue in its own right; but I also find it a useful illustration of how and why smart people say foolish things about the economy.

I'm eventually going to get around to some specifics about what the four-percenters have to say, but let me start with some general conceptual issues. Here's a question you probably don't ask yourself very often, but should: What gives Alan Greenspan such power? I don't mean why does he rule the Fed; I mean why do the decisions of the Fed's Open Market Committee—a group of charisma-impaired economists and bankers sitting around a table every six weeks—matter so much?

To answer a question like that, you need some kind of *model* of the role of monetary policy. So let me spend a few minutes laying out such a model.

At this point you are thinking "Oh no! He's going to start in with equations and economic jargon!" But don't worry—it's not that kind of model. In fact, I hope this will be fun. There will, however, be a quiz on this material—so listen carefully.

The model that I find most useful for understanding what the Fed can (and can't) do is one that some of you may have seen described in my book *Peddling Prosperity*. It was originally described by Joan and Richard Sweeney in an article entitled "Monetary Theory and the Great Capitol Hill Baby-sitting Co-op Controversy."

During the seventies the Sweeneys were members of a baby-sitting co-op—a group of young couples, mostly working on Capitol Hill, who agreed to baby-sit for each others' children on a rotating basis. Any such group, once it goes beyond a few members, requires some sort of system to make sure that each couple does its fair share. This particular co-op settled on a scrip system:

Members were issued coupons worth one hour of baby-sitting time. When a couple went out for an evening, the baby-sittees would give the appropriate number of coupons to the baby-sitters, who would then be able to "spend" them on some other occasion. The system, as you can see, was self-policing: Over time each couple would necessarily give as many hours of baby-sitting as it got.

Now if you think about it, a system like this requires that there be a fair bit of scrip in circulation. A couple might want to go out several times in close succession, and might find itself unable to take the time (or find the opportunity) to baby-sit and earn more coupons in between. Furthermore, a couple might be uncertain about its schedule, proving a further incentive to keep a reserve of scrip on hand. So on average, for the baby-sitting co-op to work properly, there needed to be quite a few coupons in circulation per couple.

I don't want to get into the fairly complicated details of how scrip was issued. Suffice it to say that after a while the co-op got into a situation in which there weren't enough coupons out there. This had some peculiar effects. Couples became reluctant to go out for the evening—because the typical couple did not have much of a reserve of baby-sitting coupons, and was anxious to keep that reserve for an important occasion. In order to build up their reserves, couples tried to do extra baby-sitting—but one couple's decision to go out was another's opportunity to baby-sit, so chances to earn coupons by baby-sitting became hard to find; and so couples became even more reluctant to spend their reserves of coupons by going out. Eventually the co-op consisted largely of couples sitting glumly at home, unwilling to go out until they had more coupons, unable to earn more coupons because nobody else was going out either.

In short, the baby-sitting co-op had managed to get itself into a recession.

Most of the members of the co-op were lawyers, so it was hard for the economists in the group to convince them that the problem was essentially monetary. Instead, the initial reaction of the co-op's officers was to treat the problem as something to be solved by regulation: For example, they tried to enforce a rule that *required* each couple to go out at least twice a month. Eventually, however, the economists prevailed, and more coupons were distributed.

The results were astonishing: With larger reserves of scrip, couples became more willing to go out, which made it easier to get opportunities to baby-sit, which made people still more willing to go out, and so on. The GBP—the gross baby-sitting-co-op product, measured in units of babies sat—soared. Of course the co-op then went on to overdo it, issuing too *many* coupons. That led to new problems, and incipient signs of inflation . . .

I warned you that there would be a quiz. So here it is—just one question: How did you feel about my telling you that story?

If your answer was "Well, that was a cute story, but I don't see what it can have to do with the U.S. economy," you get a D. You have failed to understand the usefulness of simplified models in cutting through the complexity of the real world.

If your answer was "What's all this about? I want to talk about globalization and the new information economy, and he's telling me about baby-sitting," you get an F. Not only don't you understand the uses of models, but you have fallen into the naive error of supposing that the way to be sophisticated about economics is to use big words and talk about big things.

For the fact is that by studying our model—the baby-sitting co-op, which is like a miniature version of the real U.S. economy, in which Alan Greenspan controls the supply of coupons—we can gain some very important insights that many people who believe that they are knowledgeable about these things never do seem to grasp. Let me emphasize two insights in particular.

First, we learn that there is a fundamental difference between the kind of growth associated with an increase in the money supply and the sources of longer-term growth in the economy. When GBP surged after the issuance of new coupons, it wasn't because the couples in the co-op had installed new high-tech baby-sitting equipment, or because they had been retrained to be effective in the new global baby-sitting economy, or because they had been freed from the burden of government regulations and taxes that frustrated private sector baby-sitting initiative. All that happened was that a failure of coordination due to inadequate liquidity was cured by increasing the money supply—end of story.

Second, as soon as we think about the baby-sitting story we realize that there are limits to monetary policy. Too little money is a bad thing; but while GBP could be expanded up to a point by printing more coupons, this process could only go so far. Indeed, issuing too many coupons actually hurt the co-op: an excessively expansionary monetary policy is counterproductive.

Now surely these two insights apply to the full-scale, adult economy as well. Business-cycle recoveries like 1982–1989 or 1992–1994, in which the Fed pumps money into a depressed economy and brings idle capacity back into use, tell us very little about the kind of growth that the economy can achieve on a sustained basis. Anyone who says that the Reagan-era recovery is an indicator of the kind of long-term growth that our economy could achieve if only we would institute a flat tax has simply failed to learn one lesson of the baby-sitting co-op. Anyone who thinks that the Fed can arbitrarily choose a rate of growth as a target, and achieve it indefinitely, has failed to learn the other lesson.

Can we be more specific? Indeed we can. In the U.S. economy, it is quite easy to separate cyclical fluctuations in output from the long-term growth in the economy's potential. For the past twenty years it has been quite reliably true that whenever the economy grows faster than 2.5 percent, the unemployment rate falls (about half a point for every extra point of growth), while whenever the economy grows more slowly than 2.5 percent, the unemployment rate rises. This is a pretty solid indication that the economy's potential output is growing at about 2.5 percent per year. And there is no sign whatsoever in recent data that this underlying rate of growth has accelerated—if anything, it has slipped a bit due to slower labor force growth.

The limits to expansion are harder to pin down. But we know there must be a limit *somewhere*—the baby-sitting co-op tells us so. After thirty years of intense debate, and hundreds of statistical studies, most economists have come to agree that inflation will spiral upward if the Fed tries to push unemployment too low. How low is too low? Past experience suggests that the red line—the infamous NAIRU (non-accelerating-inflation rate of unemployment)—is an unemployment rate in the 5.5 to 6 percent range; but as I'll explain in a second, the precise number is not crucial for the debate with the four-percenters.

Now, armed with our model, let's talk about what the Fed's critics have been saying. In particular, what do we make of it when someone advocates a growth target of 4 percent per year for the next five years?

Well, bear in mind that the rate of growth of potential output is reliably estimated to be less than 2.5 percent per year, and that every extra point of growth reduces the unemployment rate by half a percentage point. It immediately follows, then, that 4 percent growth for five years would mean targeting an eventual unemployment rate of something like 1.5 percent.

Now I don't know anyone who thinks that is a plausible goal. Maybe you think the NAIRU is 5 percent, not 5.5; maybe you even think that it's 4.5, though that seems grossly inconsistent with the statistical evidence. But *1.5* percent? So how can smart people think that a 4 percent growth target is feasible? Well, I've had discussions with pro-growth types myself, and have had reports from other economists who have tried to have such discussions, so here is an outline of how the discussion goes.

The first thing they say is that the old rules no longer apply, because we have had a "productivity revolution." The economy's productive potential, we are told, is now growing much faster than in the past.

What's wrong with this claim? Well, for what it's worth the numbers produced by the Bureau of Economic Analysis, which estimates productivity, do not show anything that looks like a productivity revolution. To be sure, many businessmen claim that the numbers are wrong (although there are some independent reasons to suspect that productivity growth remains fairly pedestrian). But in any case such claims don't help the pro-growth argument. The reason is that the *same* numbers are used to estimate productivity growth and GDP growth. If you think that productivity is really growing at 3 percent, not the 1 percent the BEA reports, then you must also believe that GDP is really growing at 4 percent, not 2—in other words, the Fed is *already* giving us 4 percent growth, so what's your problem? (By the way, I am told on unreliable hearsay that economists at the Fed have tried to explain this point to prominent four-percenters, and met a blank wall of incomprehension).

The second argument that growth advocates usually produce is the claim that globalization—the new openness of the U.S. economy to imports—now prevents any resurgence of inflation. This can sound plausible—but only if you don't know recent economic history, and don't think too hard about it. How can anyone think that being an economy open to trade ensures against inflation, when they have the example of Britain to contemplate? In the late 1980s Britain—a nation with a share of imports in GDP almost three times that of the United States—allowed its monetary policy to be guided by wishful thinking about how much the economy could be expanded. The result was right out of the textbook: an explosion of inflation, which was brought under control only by a return to double-digit unemployment rates.

Moreover, how can you discuss globalization without noticing that the *U.S.* has a floating exchange rate? If the Fed were to pursue a radically more expansionary monetary policy, one sure consequence would be a lower value of the dollar. If you really think that U.S. prices are basically limited by foreign competition, then you have to believe that a fall in the dollar will translate almost directly into higher inflation. In fact, traditional analyses of inflation in trading economies conclude that expansionary monetary policy has *more*, not less, effect on inflation in a country with a large import share and a floating exchange rate than it does in a relatively self-sufficient economy.

So neither productivity growth nor globalization make sense as arguments for looser monetary policy. Maybe there are other arguments—but people like Felix Rohatyn have not produced them. In short, this is not a serious debate: Although the four-percenters command a lot of political and business support, intellectually they have failed to make even the ghost of a case for their views.

Now you may think that what I am saying is that these guys are dumb—that as Bob Dole might put it, Paul Krugman thinks that he is smarter than Felix Rohatyn. But of course I'm not—after all, if I'm so smart, how come I'm not rich? No, the puzzle is why smart people say foolish things. Why haven't the four-percenters managed to make a better case? What's their model?

The answer, of course, is that they have no model. What's wrong with the kind of economics that Felix Rohatyn and many others practice is that they have failed to understand the principle. They think that you do economics the way a lawyer prepares a brief for a client—first you decide on your opinion, then you marshall as many plausible arguments as you can in support. And they imagine that the orthodoxies of economics—like the belief that the U.S. economy's potential growth rate is only 2.5 percent, or that free trade is a good thing—were arrived at in the same way.

But that's not how serious economics is done. A real economist starts not with a policy view but with a *story about how the world works.* That story almost always takes the form of a model—a simplified representation of the world, which helps you cut through the complexities. Once you have a model, you can ask how well it fits the facts; if it fits them reasonably well, you can ask what sorts of magnitudes, what sort of tradeoffs, it implies. Your policy opinions then flow from the model, not the other way around. The reason economists at the Fed think that the economy can't achieve 4 percent growth is not because they like slow growth, or because they are locked into a mindless orthodoxy: it is because they have a model of the U.S. economy that fits the facts very well and that tells them that 4 percent is a completely unrealistic target. They might be wrong—but to make a credible case for much faster growth you must counter the orthodox model with a better model, or you are engaged in an exercise in rhetoric rather than economics.

Let me also say something else. Anyone who has ever made the effort to understand a really useful economic model (like the simple models on which economists base their argument for free trade) learns something important: The model is often smarter than you are. What I mean by that is that the act of putting your thoughts together into a coherent model often forces you into conclusions you never intended, forces you to give up fondly held beliefs. The result is that people who have understood even the simplest, most trivial-sounding economic models are often far more sophisticated than people who know thousands of facts and hundreds of anecdotes, who can use plenty of big words, but have no coherent framework to organize their thoughts. If you really understood my story about the baby-sitting co-op, congratulations: You now know more about the nature of monetary policy and the business cycle than 99 percent of the attendees at Renaissance Weekend. If you have taken the time to understand the story about England trading cloth for Portuguese wine that we teach to every freshman in Econ 1, I guarantee you that you know more about the nature of the global economy than the current U.S. Trade Representative (or most of his predecessors).

I might as well raise another point. One thing that usually happens when I try to talk about the difference between serious economics and the kind of glib rhetoric that passes for sophistication is that people accuse me of being arrogant, of thinking that I know everything. I can't imagine why. No, seriously—think about it. What someone like Felix Rohatyn is in effect saying is "I don't need to make an effort to understand where the conventional views of economists come from; I don't need to understand the stuff that's in every undergraduate textbook; I'm such a smart guy that I can make up my own version of macroeconomics off the top of my head, and it will be much better than anything *they* have come up with." Then along comes this irritating economist who points out a few gaping holes in his argument, basic errors that anyone who *had* bothered to understand the stuff in the undergraduate textbook would not have made. And people's response is "That Krugman—he's so arrogant."

Well, what can we do about this kind of thing? Let me be the first to admit that economists have not made it easy for smart people who don't want to get too deep into the technicalities to understand the basics. Mathematics is a wonderful tool, but there are far too few attempts to explain the fundamental models of economics with a minimum of math; we need to make a real effort to write in English, and skip the differential topology. I'm trying, but the profession has a long way to go.

But it's also important for non-economists—people who want to be sophisticated about economic policy without getting Ph.D.s—to make an effort. As I said earlier, it's not a matter of time, it's a matter of attitude. The biggest problem with many businesspeople, political leaders, and others is that while they are willing to talk and read about economics ad nauseam, they are not willing to do anything that feels like going back to school. They would rather read five books by David Halberstam than one chapter in an undergraduate textbook; and they absolutely hate the idea that they need to work their way through whimsical stories about cloth and wine and baby-sitting rather than get right into pontificating about globalization and the new economy.

But there is no way around it. If you want to be truly well-informed about economics (or anything else), you must go back to school—and keep going back, again and again. You must be prepared to work through little models before you can use the big words—in fact, it is usually a good idea to try to avoid the big words altogether. If you balk at this task—if you think that you are too grown-up for this sort of thing—then you may sound impressive and sophisticated, but you will have no idea what you are talking about.

# *A Good Word for Inflation*

Many years ago, Paul Samuelson memorably cautioned against basing economic policy on "shibboleths," by which he meant slogans that take the place of hard thinking. Strictly speaking, this was an incorrect use of the word: The OED defines a shibboleth as "A catchword or formula adopted by a party or sect, by which their adherents or followers may be discerned, or those not their followers may be excluded." But in a deeper sense Samuelson proba-

Excerpted from "Fast Growth and Stable Prices: Just Say No," *Economist*, August 1996.

bly had it right: Simplistic ideas in economics often become badges of identity for groups of like-minded people, who repeat certain phrases to each other, and eventually mistake repetition for self-evident truth.

Public discussion of monetary policy is increasingly dominated by two such sects. The shibboleth of one sect is "growth"; that of the other is "stable prices." Those who belong to neither sect find it hard to get a hearing; indeed, journalists and politicians often seem baffled by economists who do not fit into these categories. Surely you must believe either that central banks should aim for zero inflation to the exclusion of all other goals (and that stable prices will bring huge economic benefits) or that central banks should stop worrying about inflation altogether and go for growth (and that by so doing they can bring back the growth rates of the 1960s).

But we need not make this choice. We can and should reject both fatuous promises of easy growth and mystical faith in the virtues of stable prices.

"Four Percent Follies" made the case against growth; so let me make myself even more unpopular, by making the case against stable prices.

The Economic Growth and Stability Act, proposed in 1995 by Senator Connie Mack, declares that price stability "is a key condition to maintaining the highest possible levels of productivity, real incomes, living standards, employment and global competititiveness," and enjoins the Federal Reserve to make such stability its primary goal. It's a confident declaration: You would never guess that there is hardly any reason to believe that it is true.

The fact, however, is that the costs of inflation at the low single-digit rates that now prevail in advanced countries have proved theoretically and empirically elusive. Very high inflation, which leads people into costly efforts to avoid holding cash, is one thing; but we are not remotely in that situation. Moreover, it is fairly certain that the costs of inflation, such as they are, are nonlinear in the actual rate: 3 percent inflation does much less than one-third as much harm as 9 percent.

Still, even if the gains from price stability are nowhere near as large as Senator Mack imagines, why not go for them? Because to do so would be very expensive. The great disinflation of the 1980s, which brought inflation rates down from around 10 percent to around 4, was achieved only through a prolonged period of high unemployment rates and excess capacity—in the United States, the unemployment rate did not fall back to its 1979 level until 1988, and the cumulative loss of output was more than a trillion dollars. There is every reason to expect that a push to zero inflation would involve a comparable "sacrifice ratio"—that it would cost as much as half a trillion dollars in foregone output to wring the remaining 3 points or so of inflation out of the system. This is a huge short-term pain for a small and elusive long-term gain.

And even this may not be the whole story: There is some evidence that a push to zero inflation may lead not just to a temporary sacrifice of output but to a permanently higher rate of unemployment. This is still controversial—the standard view, embodied in the concept of the NAIRU (non-accelerating-inflation rate of unemployment) is that there is no long-run tradeoff between inflation and unemployment—but recent work by George Akerlof, William Dickens, and George Perry makes a compelling case that this no-tradeoff view breaks down at very low inflation rates.

The NAIRU hypothesis is based on the reasonable proposition that people can figure out the effects of inflation—that both workers and employers realize that an 11 percent wage increase in the face of 10 percent inflation is the same thing as a 6 percent increase in the face of 5 percent inflation, and therefore that any sustained rate of inflation will simply get built into price and wage decisions. There is overwhelming evidence that this hypothesis is right—that 10 percent inflation does not buy a long-term unemployment rate significantly lower than that which can be sustained with 5 percent inflation.

But suppose that the inflation rate is very low, and that market forces are "trying" to reduce the real wages of some workers. (Even if average real wages are rising, there will usually be some industries and some categories of labor in which real wages must decline in order to maintain full employment). Is a 2 percent wage increase in the face of 5 percent inflation the same thing as a 3 percent wage fall in the face of stable prices? To hyperrational workers, it might be; but common sense suggests that in practice there is a big psychological difference between a wage rise that fails to keep pace with inflation and an explicit wage reduction. Akerlof, Dickens, and Perry have produced compelling evidence that workers are indeed very reluctant to accept nominal wage cuts: The distribution of nominal wage changes shows very few actual declines but a large concentration at precisely zero, a clear indication that there are a substantial number of workers whose real wages "should" be falling more rapidly than the inflation rate but cannot because to do so would require unacceptable nominal wage cuts.

This nominal wage rigidity means that trying to get the inflation rate very low impairs real wage flexibility, and therefore increases the unemployment rate even in the long run. Consider, for example, the case of Canada, a nation whose central bank is intensely committed to the goal of price stability (the current inflation rate is less than 1 percent). In the 1960s Canada used to have about the same unemployment rate as the United States. When it started to run persistently higher rates in the 1970s and 1980s, many economists attributed the differential to a more generous unemployment insurance system. But even as that system has become less generous, the unemployment gap has continued to widen—Canada's current rate is 10 percent. Why? The Canadian economist Pierre Fortin points out that from 1992 to 1994 a startling 47 percent of his country's collective bargaining agreements involved wage freezes—that is, precisely zero nominal wage change. Most economists would agree that high-unemployment economies like Canada suffer from inadequate real wage flexibility; Fortin's evidence suggests, however, that the cause of that inflexibility lies not in structual, microeconomic problems but in the Bank of Canada's excessive anti-inflationary zeal.

In short, the belief that absolute price stability is a huge blessing, that it brings large benefits with few if any costs, rests not on evidence but on faith. The evidence actually points strongly the other way: The benefits of price stability are elusive, the costs of getting there are large, and zero inflation may not be a good thing even in the long run.

Suppose you reject both the miracle cures of the growth sect and the old-time religion of the stable-price sect. What policies would you advocate?

A shibboleth-free policy might look like this: First, adopt as an ultimate target fairly low but not zero inflation, say 3 or 4 percent. This is high enough to accommodate most of the real wage cuts that markets impose, while the costs of the inflation itself will still be very small. However, monetary policy affects inflation only with a long lag, so it is necessary to have some more operational intermediate target. A reasonable strategy is to try to stabilize unemployment around your best estimate of the level consistent with stable inflation at the desired rate, even while recognizing that such estimates are imperfect and that the structure of the economy changes over time in any case; so you should be prepared to adjust the target unemployment rate gradually down or up if inflation performance is better or worse than you expected. And of course if past misjudgments have caused inflation to move above—or below!—the target range, policy must endeavor to bring it back into line.

This policy proposal will presumably bring angry objections

from both sides. The growth sect will denounce it as an acceptance of defeat, insisting that we need higher growth to raise living standards and solve our budget problems. Unfortunately, economics is not only about what you want—it is also about what you can get. Growth may be good, but achieving it requires more than simply declaring inflation dead.

Meanwhile, the stable-price sect will denounce this strategy as irresponsible, a return to the bad old inflationary ways of the 1970s. But the strategy is not outlandish—on the contrary, it is intended to be a description of the actual policies followed by several of the world's major central banks. In particular, what I have descibed is very close to the behavior predicted by the "Taylor rule," which successfully tracks the policies of the Federal Reserve. (It is ironic that the Fed, whose policies are in fact more growth- and employment-oriented than any other Western central bank, is the target of most of the growth sect's attacks.) But the strategy described is also arguably a pretty good description of the behavior of other central banks, including the Bank of England and—dare we say it?—the Bundesbank, which talks a monetarist game but rarely meets its own announced targets.

Of course these sensible central banks will deny that they follow any such strategy. This is understandable. Anyone who has watched the press pounce on a novice central banker naive enough to speak plainly realizes why more experienced hands, however well-intentioned and clear-headed, prefer to cloak their actions in obscurantism and hypocrisy. But while hypocrisy has its uses, it also has its dangers—above all, the danger that you may start to believe the things you hear yourself saying. This is not a hypothetical possibility. Right now there are important central banks—the Banks of Canada and France are the obvious examples—which really seem to believe what they say about wanting stable prices; their sincerity is costing their nations hundreds of thousands of jobs.

It is disturbingly easy to imagine a future in which each of the great monetary shibboleths becomes the basis of policy in a major part of the advanced world. In the United States, powerful groups on both left and right now propagandize incessantly for the belief that we can grow our problems away; aside from creating the possibility that we will rediscover the joys of stagflation, this campaign seriously weakens our already faltering resolve to put our fiscal house in order. But the bigger risk is probably in Europe, where—despite a far worse employment performance than in the United States—the rhetoric of price stability goes largely unchallenged, and is likely to have growing influence over actual policy.

In particular, what will happen if EMU comes to pass? The new European Central Bank will operate under a constitution that honors price stability above all else; more important, it will feel that it must demonstrate itself a worthy successor to the Bundesbank, which means that it will try to implement in practice the kind of policy the Bundesbank follows only in theory. The result will be that Europe's unemployment problem, which would be severe in any case, will be seriously aggravated.

Shibboleths make people feel good. Not only are they an alternative to the pain of hard thinking, but because so many people repeat them, they offer a reassuring sense of community. But we must go beyond the shibboleths, however comfortable they make us feel: Monetary policy is too serious a business to be conducted on the basis of simplistic slogans.

# *What Is Wrong with Japan?*

When the world's second largest economy, after forty years of impressive economic growth, stagnates for six years with no real recovery in sight, one would think that people would regard the causes of that economic stagnation as a truly burning issue. Yet even now there is a strange casualness in the way that most people—including, unfortunately, many Japanese—discuss the nation's problems. Instead of a serious, thoughtful analysis, all one usually hears is a long list of things wrong with Japan. The

Originally published in *Nihon Keizai Shimbun*.

country, we are told, has a weak financial sector; it is overregulated; there is not enough competition; Japanese firms are moving production to Southeast Asia; and so on. All of these things are true; nonetheless, a list is not the same as a real analysis. And in fact the tendency to explain Japan's problems in terms of a long list of factors does real harm, because it encourages a sort of fatalism in the face of economic stagnation. After all, if there are so many problems, we cannot expect a quick fix.

The truth, however, is that matters are not that complicated. Japan has many problems—but what country does not? The main obstacle to Japanese recovery right now is not the long list of structural difficulties but a simple lack of clear thinking and courage.

For one thing, most of the items on everybody's list of what is wrong with Japan are things that make the economy inefficient. That is, all of these things reduce the ability of the economy to produce goods and services—they limit its supply capacity. But the immediate problem with the Japanese economy is not too little supply—it is too little demand. The problem is that the economy isn't using the production capacity it already has—a problem for which many of the items on the usual list are simply irrelevant.

Now as a general rule modern economies are not supposed to suffer from prolonged periods of inadequate demand. There is usually nothing easier than increasing demand: Just have the central bank (i.e., the Bank of Japan) increase the money supply, or have the government spend more. Why, then, has Japan suffered from low demand for more than half a decade?

Well, there are some structural reasons. Japanese consumers still save an unusually high fraction of their income, which means that companies must correspondingly be persuaded to maintain a high investment rate if the economy is not to have too little demand. The problem is aggravated because the troubles of the banking system have restricted the flow of credit. So to push demand high enough to get the economy back to more or less full use of its capacity would require a big stimulus. Still, why not provide that stimulus?

The standard answer goes like this: Interest rates are already very low, so the Bank of Japan has done all it can. Meanwhile, the government has a severe fiscal problem, so it cannot increase spending or cut taxes. There is, in short, nothing to be done except pursue structural reforms and hope for an eventual turnaround.

This answer sounds hard-headed and responsible. In fact, however, it is based on a completely false premise—the idea that the Bank of Japan has reached the limits of what it can do.

The simple fact is that there is no limit on how much a central bank can increase the supply of money. Could the Bank of Japan, for example, double the amount of monetary base—that is, bank reserves plus cash in circulation—over the next year? Sure: just buy that amount of Japanese government debt. True, even such a large increase in the money supply might not drive down interest rates very much, since they are already so low. But an increase in Japan's money supply could ease the economic problem in ways other than lower interest rates. It is possible that putting more cash in circulation will stimulate spending directly—that the extra money will simply "burn holes in people's pockets." Or banks, awash in reserves, might become more willing to lend; or individuals, with all that cash on hand, will bypass the banks and find other ways of investing. And even if none of these things happens, when the Bank of Japan increases the monetary base it does so by buying off government debt—and therefore makes room for spending increases or tax cuts.

So never mind those long lists of reasons for Japan's slump. The answer to the country's immediate problems is simple: PRINT LOTS OF MONEY.

But won't that be inflationary? Well, remember that the Bank of Japan is supposed to be impotent: If it prints more money, people will simply hoard it rather than spend it. But printing money is only inflationary if people spend it, and if that spending exceeds the economy's capacity to produce. You cannot first argue that monetary policy is ineffective as a way to increase demand, then reject a proposal to print more money on the grounds that it will cause inflation.

So why doesn't the Bank of Japan just go out and print lots of money? The best theory I have heard is that the bureaucrats at the Bank of Japan and the Ministry of Finance are still mesmerized by the memory of the "bubble economy"—the wild speculation of the late 1980s, which pushed the prices of stocks and real estate to crazy levels (remember when the grounds of the Imperial Palace were supposedly worth more than the whole state of California?). They believe that loose monetary policy created that bubble—which may be true—and that the bursting of the bubble caused the slump of the 1990s—which may also be true. And so they are afraid to increase the money supply now for fear of repeating the experience.

There is an old joke that may be useful here: A driver runs over a pedestrian, who is left lying in the road behind his car. He looks back and says "I am so sorry—let me undo the damage"—and proceeds to back up his car, running over the pedestrian a second time. Japan's economic managers are acting like that driver. They do not realize that 1997 is not 1987, and that doing the opposite of what they did then only compounds the country's problems.

# *Seeking the Rule of the Waves*

Books that propound theories of history—that is, that claim to find common patterns in events widely separated in time and space—have a deservedly dicey reputation among the professionals. When such books are good they can be very good: A classic like William McNeill's *Plagues and Peoples* can permanently change the way you look at human affairs. Most bigthink books about history, however, turn out to offer little more than strained analogies mixed with pretentious restatements of the obvious; a few have been downright pernicious.

Originally published in *Foreign Affairs*, May/June 1997.

Still, the public has a powerful and understandable appetite for theories that seem to explain it all, and so they keep on coming. David Hackett Fischer's *The Great Wave: Price Revolutions and the Rhythm of History* has already generated considerable buzz. Remarkably for a book that spends most of its five-hundred-plus pages dwelling on events centuries (and occasionally millennia) in the past, a good deal of the buzz comes from the business community, not usually noted for its interest in history. Indeed, Fischer is getting favorable mention from people who tell us in the next breath that we live in a New Economy to which old rules no longer apply.

There is a reason for this peculiar affinity between a historian with an eight-century perspective and business commentators obsessed with the new; what these pundits really want, it turns out, is to use his account of alleged patterns in the distant past as an excuse to ignore the lessons of more recent history.

Fischer's book looks promising on the face of it. Inflation is a plausible candidate for a far-ranging search for parallels and common principles. And the book also starts well, with a stirring and eloquent defense of the role of quantification in history (although my favorite along these lines is still Colin McEvedy's introduction to *The Penguin Atlas of Ancient History*, which contains this immortal sentence: "History being a branch of the biological sciences, its ultimate expression must be mathematical."). I plan to keep *The Great Wave* on my shelf both as a useful source of facts and figures and as a guide to data sources; the author did do a lot of homework.

It is therefore a shame that the book turns out, in the end, to be quite wrong-headed. But let us not be too harsh: It is wrong-headed in interesting ways, and we can learn quite a lot by examining how and where Fischer went astray.

Fischer starts with an empirical observation: If you look at the history of prices in the Western world since the twelfth century, you can broadly divide that history into alternating periods of generally rising prices and of rough price stability. Everyone knows that the twentieth century has been an era of inflation, and the prolonged price rise from 1500 to 1700 is also well known; Fischer makes a good case, however, that there were also reasonably well-defined eras of price increase in pre–Black Death medieval Europe and in the eighteenth century.

What does conventional economic history have to say about these "price revolutions"? Well, the two familiar ones are both generally attributed to increases in the supply of money, but with those increases themselves driven by very different factors. The long inflation from 1500 to 1700 is mainly attributed to the flood of silver from Spain's New World conquests; in the modern world governments can print money instead of mining it, and have done so repeatedly both to pay their bills and, more creditably, in an attempt to trade off higher prices for lower unemployment.

Fischer regards such explanations as inadequate. He insists both that inflation is only one symptom of a deeper process—one that also produces growing population, rising inequality, declining real wages, and ultimately a crisis—and that this process is repetitive, that in a qualitative sense all price revolutions are alike. In particular, the travails of the West in recent decades are typical of the end game of a price revolution—and we can take comfort from the fact that such difficult periods are inevitably followed by a prolonged "equilibrium."

This thesis is both fun to contemplate and comforting in its implication that the worst may already be behind us. What is wrong with it? One problem with *The Great Wave* is that Fischer shares a common shortcoming of historical writers on matters economic: He would clearly rather spend a year hunting down facts than a day mastering a theory, even if only to learn enough to reject it. As a result, his accounts of what he imagines to be the conventional theories of inflation—theories that he claims to refute with his evidence—are wildly off-base, sometimes ludicrously so.

Fischer's impatience with analytical thinking extends to his own ideas; the book contains quite a few whoppers, assertions that fall apart if given even a moment's serious thought. An illuminating example involves his discussion of the origins of the great price rise after 1500. He points out correctly that prices in Europe began rising well before New World silver began to arrive—which he argues refutes any monetarist explanation. But there is no mystery here: As he admits, there was a surge in European silver production in the late fifteenth century, mainly from mines in Bohemia and Southern Germany. (Coins stamped at one of those mines, at Joachimsthal, were circulated so widely that "thaler" became a generic phrase for any silver coin—and eventually, with some slippage in spelling and pronunciation, for pieces of green paper bearing George Washington's portrait.) Fischer insists, however, that the rise in European silver production was a result rather than a cause of inflation—that mines were opened and expanded to meet the "desperate need for liquidity" produced by rising prices.

Think about that for a minute. We can be sure that fifteenth-century German mineowners neither knew nor cared about Europe's need for liquidity—they were simply trying to make a profit. Now ask yourself: Does inflation (a rise in the price of goods and services in terms of silver) make it more or less profitable to open a silver mine? The clear answer is that it makes the mine *less* profitable: A pound of silver extracted from the mine would buy fewer goods and services than before. Had Fischer devoted even a few minutes to thinking his story through, he would have realized that. Yet the claim that rising prices necessarily induce increased creation of money is crucial to his whole theory.

There is, however, an even bigger problem with *The Great Wave*. Like most efforts to derive lessons for the present from the broad sweep of history, Fischer's thesis essentially involves denying that the Industrial Revolution led to any fundamental change in the way the world works. But the fact is that beginning in the eighteenth century there *was* a qualitative change in the nature not only of economic life but of human society in general, a change more profound than any since the rise of civilization itself. That does not mean that we have nothing to learn from earlier centuries; it does mean that we have to be very careful in drawing parallels.

There are many ways in which the preindustrial world was another planet from the one we now inhabit, but let me focus on two changes that are particularly crucial in this context.

First, for fifty-five out of the last fifty-seven centuries Malthus was right. What I mean is that for almost all of the history of civilization improvements in technology did not lead to sustained increases in living standards; instead, the gains were dissipated by rising population, with pressure on resources eventually driving the condition of the masses back to roughly its previous level. The subjects of Louis XIV were not noticeably better nourished than those of ancient Sumerian city-states; that is, while they had enough to survive and raise children in good times, they lived sufficiently close to the edge that the Four Horsemen could carry them off now and then, keeping the population more or less stable.

It was Malthus's great misfortune that the power of his theory to explain what happened in most of human history has been obscured by the fact that the only two centuries of that history for which it does not work happen to be the two centuries that followed its publication. But this was, of course, not an accident. Malthus was a man of his time, and his musings were only one symptom of the rise of a rationalist, scientific outlook; another symptom of that rise was the Industrial Revolution.

Because Malthus was right, however, the Great Waves of economic activity in the preindustrial world, while they undoubtedly existed, were driven by forces that have little relevance to more recent fluctuations. In particular, the most important discipline for understanding long swings in preindustrial population and real wages is not macroeconomics but microbe economics. Now and then devastating new diseases would appear (often, as McNeill showed in *Plagues and Peoples*, as a result either of conquests or of the opening of new trade routes, both of which tended to bring formerly separated populations, and the germs that they harbored, into contact). Initially the population would plunge and real wages would soar. As microbes and humans coevolved into a new equilibrium, population and pressure on resources would rise again, and the increasingly malnourished masses would become vulnerable to the next plague. All this is fascinating; but its relevance to twenty-first-century economic prospects is questionable.

The other great change is the invention of the business cycle. Economic instability has, of course, always been with us. But economic downturns before 1800 were the result of "supply-side" events such as harvest failures and wars. They bore little resemblance to modern recessions, which are the result of slumps in monetary demand. To have a recession as we understand it today, you must have a structure of paper credit erected on top of or in place of the circulation of gold and silver—otherwise, the credit contraction so central to the phenomenon cannot get started in the first place. And you must also have a substantial part of the economy that is likely to respond to slumping demand by cutting production rather than prices—otherwise a financial contraction will lead to deflation, but not to an actual decline in output. Preindustrial economies could not have recessions as we know them, both because of the simplicity of their monetary systems and because they consisted mostly of farmers, who respond to a drop in demand mainly by cutting prices rather than by growing less.

Economic historians generally think that the first true recession was the slump that hit England after the end of the Napoleonic Wars—in other words, the first recession occurred, as one would expect, in the first industrial nation. Nations that industrialized later also had to wait for their chance to share the recession experience. My colleague, the distinguished economic historian Peter Temin, tells me that the United States did not experience a true recession until the Panic of 1873. Moreover, he has produced evidence that between 1820 and 1860 there was a clear difference in the behavior of the U.S. and U.K. economies: America was still a "classical" economy in which financial contractions might reduce prices but had little effect on growth, while England was already beginning to look recognizably Keynesian.

And that brings us both to the reason why people in the business community think that Fischer's book is relevant to current events, and to the reason why it is in fact not relevant at all.

Anyone who reads the business press knows that the mood these days is one of what-me-worry optimism. After six years of fairly steady growth with surprisingly quiescent inflation, every major newspaper and magazine has either suggested or flatly declared that the business cycle is dead—that the recession of 1990–1991 was the last such slump we will see for many years to come.

Nay-sayers like myself try to puncture this serenity by insisting that it ignores the lessons of history. It was not that long ago that George Bush got the boot because of the economy, stupid; we had a truly vicious recession in the early 1980s; and for that matter Mexico, Japan, and even Canada (remember them? they're that country next to us) can attest that the nineties have by no means been always and everywhere as placid as the last few years in the United States. Moreover, we've been here before: Near the end of another long recovery, in the late 1960s, pronouncements that the business cycle was dead were just as prevalent as they are today.

Why does the business cycle persist? Because, as the bumper stickers don't quite say, stuff happens: The world refuses to stay put, and policy is always playing catch-up. To look at the causes of booms and slumps since the last time the business cycle was declared dead is to be awed at the sheer variety of curve balls history manages to throw at us. Who in 1969 imagined that a recession could be triggered by a war in the Middle East—let alone a fundamentalist revolution in Iran? Who would have thought that the ever-so-controlled Japanese economy could be whipsawed by a financial bubble that drove land and stock prices to ridiculous levels, then burst? Who could have predicted that two well-meaning projects—the political unification of Germany, and the monetary unification of Europe—would interact to produce a disastrous slump? True, we learn from experience: The stock market crash of 1987 didn't play like that of 1929, because this time Alan Greenspan knew what to do. But as fast as we learn to cope with old sources of boom and slump, new sources emerge.

Some people tell us that the forces that used to drive many recessions have abated: We are no longer as much of a manufacturing economy, inventories have become less of an "accelerator" of slumps, and so on. And they are surely right: We will not have the same problems in the future that we had in the past. We will have different problems. And because the problems are new, we will handle them badly, and the business cycle will endure.

But this is not a message business pundits want to hear; and for them Fischer's book is the perfect answer. Of course, they can now say, the business cycle has been with us for the last 150 years—but the long view tells us that while instability is the norm while you are passing through a price revolution, it is smooth sailing once you pass through the crisis and reach the new "equilibrium." And guess what—we have just arrived at the promised land.

But the modern business cycle bears no more resemblance to the economic fluctuations that afflicted preindustrial Europe than NATO does to the Holy Roman Empire. It may be tempting to ignore the very real lessons of the last century because of some alleged parallels with the distant past. To do so, however, would be to use history not as a guide to the present, but merely as an excuse for some very ahistorical wishful thinking.

# The Speculator's Ball

The 1990s have been a great age for financial speculation. Markets have been rigged, currencies overthrown, vast sums made and lost with an abandon not seen for generations. The essays in this part try to make some sense of it all. The first essay here, "How Copper Came a Cropper," discusses the amazing story of Sumitomo's initially successful "corner" on the world copper market. The next, "The Tequila Effect," turns to a more tragic case—the havoc wreaked on Mexico and other Latin American nations by the currency crisis that erupted at the end of 1994. With "Bahtulism" we move on to the Asian currency crises of 1997; and the final piece here, "Making the World Safe for George Soros," tries to step back for a broader view, albeit one with a special European focus.

# How Copper Came a Cropper

In 1995 the world was astonished to hear that a young employee of the ancient British firm Barings had lost more than a billion dollars in speculative trading, quite literally breaking the bank. But when an even bigger financial disaster was revealed a year later—the loss of more than $3 billion in the copper market by an employee of Sumitomo Corp.—the story quickly faded from the front pages. "Oh well, just another rogue trader," was the general reaction.

It eventually became clear, however, that Yasuo Hamanaka, unlike Nick Leeson of Barings, was not a poorly supervised

Originally published in *Slate,* July 19, 1996.

employee using his company's money to gamble on unpredictable markets. On the contrary, there is little question that he was, in fact, implementing a deliberate corporate strategy of "cornering" the world copper market—a strategy that worked, yielding huge profits, for a number of years. Hubris brought him down in the end; but it is his initial success, not his eventual failure, that is the really disturbing part of the tale.

To understand what Sumitomo was up to, you don't need to know many details about the copper market. The essential facts about copper (and many other commodities) are (1) it is subject to wide fluctuations in the balance between supply and demand, and (2) it can be stored, so that production need not be consumed at once. These two facts mean that a certain amount of speculation is a normal and necessary part of the way the market works: It is inevitable and desirable that people should try to buy low and sell high, building up inventories when the price is perceived to be unusually low and running those inventories down when the price seems to be especially high.

So far so good. But a long time ago somebody—let's say a Phoenician tin merchant in the first millennium B.C.—realized that a clever man with sufficiently deep pockets could basically hold such a market up for ransom. The details are often mind-numbingly complex, but the principle is simple. Buy up a large part of the supply of whatever commodity you are trying to corner—it doesn't really matter whether you actually take claim to the stuff itself or buy up "futures," which are nothing but promises to deliver the stuff on a specified date—then deliberately keep some, not all, of what you have bought off the market, to sell later. What you have now done, if you have pulled it off, is created an artificial shortage that sends prices soaring, allowing you to make big profits on the stuff you do sell. You may be obliged to take some loss on the supplies you have withheld from the market, selling them later at lower prices, but if you do it right, this loss will be far smaller than your gain from higher current prices.

It's a beautiful idea; there are only three important hitches. First, you must be able to operate on a sufficiently large scale. Second, the strategy only works if not too many people realize what is going on—otherwise nobody will sell to you in the first place unless you offer a price so high that the game no longer pays. Third, this kind of thing is, for obvious reasons, quite illegal. (The first Phoenician who tried it probably got very rich; the second got sacrificed to Moloch.)

The amazing thing is that Sumitomo managed to overcome all these hitches. The world copper market is immense; nonetheless, a single trader, apparently, was able and willing to dominate that market. You might have thought that the kind of secrecy required for such a massive market manipulation was impossible in the modern information age—but Hamanaka pulled it off, partly by working through British intermediaries, but mainly through a covert alliance with Chinese firms (some of them state-owned). And as for the regulators . . . well, what about the regulators?

For that is the disturbing part of the Sumitomo story. If Hamanaka had really been nothing more than an employee run wild, one could not really fault regulators for failing to rein him in; that would have been his employer's job. But he wasn't; he was, in effect, engaged in a price-fixing conspiracy on his employer's behalf. And while it may not have been obvious what Sumitomo was up to early in the game, the role of "Mr. Copper" and his company in manipulating prices has apparently been common knowledge for years among everyone familiar with the copper market. Indeed, copper futures have been the object of massive speculative selling by the likes of George Soros, precisely because informed players believed that Hamanaka was keeping the price at artificially high levels, and that it would eventually plunge. (Soros, however, gave up a few months too soon, apparently intimidated by Sumitomo's seemingly limitless resources.) So why was Hamanaka allowed to continue?

The answer may in part be that the global nature of his activities made it unclear who had responsibility. Should it have been Japan, because Sumitomo is based there? Should it have been Britain, home of the London Metal Exchange? Should it have been the United States, where much of the copper Sumitomo ended up owning is warehoused? Beyond this confusion over responsibility, however, one suspects that regulators were inhibited by the uncritically pro-market ideology of our times. Many people nowadays take it as an article of faith that free markets always take care of themselves—that there is no need to police people like Hamanaka, because the market will automatically punish their presumption.

And Sumitomo's strategy did indeed eventually come to grief—but only because Hamanaka apparently could not bring himself to face the fact that even the most successful market manipulator must accept an occasional down along with the ups. Rather than sell some of his copper at a loss, he chose to play double or nothing, trying to repeat his initial success by driving prices ever higher; since a market corner is necessarily a sometime thing, his unwillingness to let go led to disaster. But had Hamanaka been a bit more flexible and realistic, Sumitomo could have walked away from the copper market with modest losses offset by enormous, ill-gotten gains.

The funny thing about the Sumitomo affair is that if you ignore the exotic trimmings—the Japanese names, the Chinese connection—it's a story right out of the robber-baron era, the days of Jay Gould and Jim Fisk. There has been a worldwide rush to deregulate financial markets, to bring back the good old days of the nineteenth century when investors were free to make money however they saw fit. Maybe the Sumitomo affair will remind us that not all the profitable things unfettered investors can do with their money are socially productive; maybe it will even remind us why we regulated financial markets in the first place.

# *The Tequila Effect*

Relations between Mexico and the United States are not what they were in the early 1990s. In the eyes of many Americans, Mexico is a corrupt nation ruled by drug lords and wracked by economic crisis. In the eyes of many Mexicans, the United States is simultaneously tyrannical and self-indulgent, imposing harsh economic medicine on its neighbor while blaming it for a drug trade that is really our own fault. The voters who turned on the ruling party in Mexico's 1997 elections were also, at least in part, showing

Originally published in *USA Today*, May 5, 1997.

their displeasure for a government too close to the United States.

And yet things could easily have been much worse. In particular, if Bill Clinton hadn't done the right thing early in 1995, Mexico's economy could have imploded, ending forever the hope of reform in that long-suffering nation.

In the months after the crushing Republican victory in the 1994 Congressional elections, much of the Clinton administration's inner circle was still in a state of stunned stupor. Yet in those dark days a handful of officials persuaded Clinton to support a daring, risky, and extremely unpopular policy initiative: the rescue, with a huge loan, of Mexico's collapsing economy. Had that initiative failed, it might well have doomed Clinton's presidency and much more besides. But it succeeded, and history may record the decision to go ahead with their plan as Clinton's finest hour.

In the early 1990s Mexico was the darling of international investors, who were convinced that the economic reforms of then-president Carlos Salinas would produce robust economic growth. The warnings of a few economists that the hype about Mexican prospects was not matched by actual performance were ignored, and money poured in at the rate of $30 billion a year. But over the course of 1994 a series of disturbing news items—a peasant rebellion, the assassination of a presidential candidate, and some bad economic statistics—made the markets increasingly nervous. Finally, in December, the number of fidgety investors reached critical mass, and there was a full-blown run on the Mexican peso.

So far this is not too unusual a story; currency crises are actually quite common, and often do little long-run harm. But it soon became apparent that Mexico was different: Having placed the nation on a pedestal for several years, investors were shocked—shocked!—to discover that the country was not a combination of Singapore and Switzerland, and began pulling their money out as blindly as they had put it in.

The exact details of what happened next are not a matter of

public record. But it seems clear that the key figure was Treasury Undersecretary (now Deputy Secretary) Lawrence Summers, a former Harvard professor who has emerged as the economic brains of the Clinton administration. Summers reached two conclusions about Mexico's crisis: that there was a chance that American intervention could make the difference between recovery and catastrophe, and that this chance was worth taking.

What Summers and others at the Treasury realized was that Mexico was plunging into a sort of political-economic death spiral. The panic of investors could not be rationalized by the weakness of the economy alone: What was driving money out of Mexico was political fear, the concern that Mexico's recent openness to foreign capital and foreign goods might be about to be reversed, that the country might revert to a populist anti-Americanism. The capital flight inspired by this fear was causing a disastrous business slump. And it was this slump that, in turn, was the most powerful cause of political unrest. In short, there was every prospect that pesssimism about Mexico's future could turn into a self-fulfilling prophecy.

The answer, as they saw it, was to give Mexico a bit of breathing room: to lend the Mexican government some money, allowing it to stay afloat and to cushion the blows falling on the private sector. If all went well this would in turn give private investors a chance to recover their nerve, and the vicious circle of decline would turn into a virtuous circle of recovery. Of course if all did not go well, the loan might not be repaid. And then there would be hell to pay. Mexico is not a small country, and a loan would do no good unless it was big enough to matter; in the event, the United States and other countries (whose elbows still hurt from the twisting we gave them) provided a credit line of $50 billion. Just imagine the public reaction if any substantial fraction of that money had been lost!

Why, then, take such a huge risk? Because Mexico is not just any country. Not only does it share a 2,000-mile border with the

United States, it is a traditionally difficult neighbor which at the moment happens to be ruled by U.S.-educated technocrats, but whose friendliness can never be taken for granted. To have "our guys" preside over an economic collapse, as seemed all too likely in early 1995, would have been a major foreign policy disaster. There was also, to be frank, the question of protecting the large sums of private money already invested in Mexico; but it is possible to be too cynical. For what it is worth, my sources say that foreign policy, not the interests of Rubin's Wall Street friends, was the decisive concern.

And so one winter day Rubin and Summers marched into the Oval Office with their plan—and, incredibly, Clinton agreed. Lending taxpayers' money to Mexico when private investors were pulling out was not a popular idea. In fact, it quickly became clear that Congress would not allocate the necessary funds; instead the Treasury engaged in some fancy footwork, exploiting a legal loophole to lend Mexico the money without Congressional approval. Furious Republicans, led by Senator Alfonse D'Amato, denounced the plan, and prepared to hang Summers from the rafters when the rescue failed.

But the rescue did not fail. Mexico's economy, after plunging 10 percent in the first year after the crisis, has recovered the lost ground. Private investors have returned, stabilizing the peso; and the Mexican government, years ahead of schedule, has repaid that emergency loan. Mexico is not yet completely out of the woods, but U.S. taxpayers are.

So what are the morals of the story? One is that sometimes it pays to listen to the experts: many people find arrogant technocrats like Larry Summers annoying, but smart is as smart does—and he did. The other is that sometimes it actually pays to do the unpopular thing: If Clinton had listened to the polls that winter day, Mexico would probably be a basket case—and Bob Dole would probably be president.

# *Bahtulism: Who Poisoned Asia's Currency Markets?*

Currency-crisis connoisseurs cherish the memory of George Brown, Britain's Secretary of Economic Affairs in the mid-1960s—the man who blamed his troubles on the "gnomes of Zurich." (He was misinformed: the relevant gnomes are actually in Basel.) But we may have to remove Brown from his pedestal, to make room for Malaysian Prime Minister Mahathir Mohamad. Last month Malaysia's neighbor Thailand, after months of promising that it wouldn't, devalued the baht, and spooked

Originally published in *Slate*, August 14, 1997.

investors began selling Malyasian ringgit (and Philippine pesos, Indonesian rupiahs, and so on) as well. This provoked an outburst on Mahathir's part that surely counts as an instant classic. Where Brown was vague about both the identity of the villains and their motives, Mahathir had a full-fledged conspiracy theory: The U.S. government had prompted palindromic speculator George Soros to undermine Asia's economies, because it wants to impose Western values (like democracy and civil rights) on them. And Mahathir's ministers expanded on his remarks with a rhetoric that was unusual for a government with a long-term interest in maintaining the goodwill of international investors: Currency fluctuations are caused by "hostile elements bent on . . . unholy actions" that constitute "villainous acts of sabotage" and "the height of international criminality."

These remarks were entertaining both because, as far as we can tell, Soros was *not* a major player in the crisis (indeed, he seems to have taken a bit of a bath by failing to anticipate this one), and because in the early 1990s one of the world's most ambitious and reckless currency speculators was . . . Malaysia's government-controlled central bank, which only got out of the business after losing nearly $6 billion.

Currency crises often provoke hysterical reactions in government officials. One day your country's economy is humming along nicely, your bonds are AAA, you have billions of dollars in foreign exchange reserves socked away. Then all of a sudden the reserves are depleted, nobody will buy your paper, and you can only keep money in the country by raising interest rates to recession-inducing levels. How can things go wrong so fast?

The standard response of economists is that to blame the financial markets in such a situation is to shoot the messenger, that a crisis is simply the market's way of telling a government that its policies aren't sustainable. You may wonder at the abruptness with which that message is delivered. But that, says the canonical model, is simply part of the logic of the situation.

To see why, forget about currencies for a minute, and imagine a government trying to stabilize the price of some commodity, such as gold. The government can do this, at least for a while, if it starts with a sufficiently large stockpile of the stuff: All it has to do is sell some of its hoard whenever the price threatens to rise about the target level.

Now suppose that this stockpile is gradually dwindling over time, so that far-sighted speculators can foresee the day—perhaps many years distant—when it will be exhausted. They will realize that this offers them an opportunity. Once the government has exhausted its stockpile, it can no longer stabilize the price—which will therefore shoot up. All they have to do, then, is to buy some of the stuff a little while before the reserves are gone, then resell it at a large capital gain.

But these speculative purchases of gold or whatever will accelerate the exhaustion of the stockpile, bringing the day of reckoning closer. So the smart speculators will try to get ahead of the crowd, buying earlier—and thereby running down the stocks even sooner, leading to still earlier purchases. . . . The result is while the government's stockpile may decline only gradually for a long time, when it falls below some critical point all hell suddenly—and predictably—breaks loose (as actually happened in the gold market during 1969).

With a bit of imagination this same story can be applied to currency crises. Imagine a government that is trying to support the dollar value of the ringgit—or, what is the same thing, to keep a lid on the price of a dollar measured in ringgit—through foreign exchange market "intervention," which basically means selling dollars to keep their ringgit price down. And suppose the government's policies are, for whatever reason, inconsistent with keeping the exchange rate fixed forever. Then there is a complete parallel with the previous story, with foreign exchange reserves taking on the role of the gold stockpile. And by the same logic as before, we can conclude that speculators will not wait for events to take their course: At some critical moment they will all move in at once—and billions of dollars in reserves may vanish in days, even hours.

The abruptness of a currency crisis, then, does not mean that it strikes out of a clear blue sky. In the standard economic model, the real villain is the inconsistency of the government's own policies.

Is Mahathir's complaint therefore unadulterated nonsense? No: As Art Buchwald once said of his own writing, it is adulterated nonsense. The truth is that speculators may not always be quite as blameless as the standard model would have it.

For one thing, markets aren't always cool, calm, and collected. There is abundant evidence that financial markets are subject to occasional bouts of what is known technically as "herding": Everyone sells because everyone else is selling. This may happen because individual investors are irrational; it may also happen because so much of the world's money is controlled by fund managers who will not be blamed if they do what everyone else is doing. One consequence of herding, however, is that a country's currency may be subjected to an unjustified selling frenzy.

It is also true that the long-run sustainability of a country's policies is to some extent a matter of opinion—and that policies that might have worked out given time may be abandoned in the face of market pressures. This leads to the possibility of self-fulfilling prophecies—for example, a competent finance minister may be fired because of a currency crisis, and the irresponsible policies of his successor end up ratifying the market's bad opinion of the country.

All of this, in turn, creates a *possible* way for private investors with big enough resources to play a nefarious financial game. Here's how it would work, in theory: Suppose that a country's currency is in a somewhat ambiguous situation—its current value might be sustainable, or it might not. A big investor quietly takes a short position in that country's currency—that is, he borrows money in pounds, or baht, or ringgit, and invests the money in some other country. Once he has a big enough position, he begins ostentatiously selling the target currency, gives interviews to the *Financial Times* about how he thinks it is vulnerable, and so on; and with luck provokes a run on the currency by other investors, forcing a devaluation that immediately reduces the value of those carefully acquired debts, but not the value of the matching assets, leaving him hundreds of millions of dollars richer.

Speculative sharp practice, in short, *can* play a role in destabilizing currencies. But how important is that role in reality?

Well, George Soros pulled the trick off in Britain in 1992; but as far as anyone knows even he has done it only once. True, it was an amazing coup: He is supposed to have made more than a billion dollars. It's also true, however, that there were good reasons for the pound's devaluation, and it is unclear whether Soros really caused the crisis or was merely smart enough to anticipate it. Maybe he brought it on a few weeks early.

The other currency crises of the nineties—and it has been a great decade for such crises—have taken place without the help of sinister financial masterminds. This is no accident; opportunities like the one Soros discovered in 1992 are rare. They require that a country's currency be clearly vulnerable, but not yet under attack—a narrow window at best, since there is a sort of Murphy's Law in these things: If something can go wrong with a currency, it usually will. Financial markets are not in the habit of giving countries the benefit of the doubt.

Does this mean that there is no defense against speculative attack? Not at all. In fact, there are two very effective ways to prevent runs on your currency. One—call it the "benign neglect" strategy—is simply to deny speculators a fixed target. Speculators can't make an easy profit betting against the U.S. dollar, because the U.S. government doesn't try to defend any particular exchange rate—which means that any obvious downside risk is already reflected in the price, and on any given day the dollar is as likely to go up as down. The other—call it the "Caesar's wife" strategy—is to make very sure that your commitment to a particular exchange rate is credible. Nobody attacks the guilder, because the Dutch clearly have both the capability and the intention of keeping it pegged to the German mark.

Oh yes—there is also a third option. You can erect elaborate regulations to keep people from moving money out of your country. Of course, if investors know that it will be hard to get money out, they will be reluctant to put it in to begin with. There is a case to be made—an unfashionable case, but not a totally crazy one—that it is worth forgoing the benefits of capital inflows in order to avoid the risk of capital outflows. But Asian leaders uttered not a word of complaint when they were receiving huge inflows of money, much of it going to dubious real estate ventures; only when irrational exuberance turned into probably rational skittishness did the accusations begin.

So Mahathir's claims that he is the victim of an American conspiracy are just plain silly. He has nobody but himself to blame for his difficulties. Or at least that's what George, Bob, and Madeleine told me to say.

## A Note on Currency Crises

I often run into people who assert confidently that massive speculative attacks on currencies like the British pound in 1992, the Mexican peso in 1994–1995, and the Thai baht in 1997 prove that we are in a new world in which computerized trading, satellite hookups, and all that, mean that old economic rules, and conventional economic theory, no longer apply. (One physicist insisted that the economy has "gone nonlinear," and is now governed by chaos theory.) But the truth is that currency crises are old hat; the travails of the

French franc in the twenties were thoroughly modern, and the speculative attacks that brought down the Bretton Woods system of exchange rates in the early seventies were almost as big compared with the size of the economies involved as the biggest recent blowouts. And currency crises have been a favorite topic of international financial economists ever since the 1970s. In fact, it is one of *my* favorite topics—after all, I helped found the field.

The standard economic model of currency crises had its genesis in a brilliant mid-seventies analysis of the gold market by Dale Henderson and Steve Salant, two economists at the Federal Reserve. They showed that abrupt speculative attacks, which would almost instantly wipe out the government's stockpile, were a natural consequence of typical price stabilization schemes. In 1977 I was an intern at the Fed, and realized that Salant and Henderson's story could, with some reinterpretation, be applied to currency crises that suddenly wipe out the government's reserves. A bit later Robert Flood, now at the IMF, and Peter Garber of Brown produced the canonical version of that conventional story.

The key lesson from that conventional model is that abrupt runs on a currency, which move billions of dollars in a very short time, are not necessarily the result either of irrational investor stampedes or of evil financial manipulation. On the contrary, they are the normal result when rational investors contemplate the implications of unsustainable policies.

Some economists, however—notably Berkeley's Maurice Obstfeld and Barry Eichengreen—argue that the standard model is too mechanical in its representation of government policy; and that the more complex motives of actual governments make speculation a more uncertain and perhaps more pernicious affair. Self-fulfilling crises, in which a currency that could have survived is nonetheless brought down, are a hot topic these days. But everyone agrees that a sufficiently credible currency will never be attacked, and a sufficiently incredible one will always come under fire.

# Making the World Safe for George Soros

The very first real paper I ever wrote in economics was a piece entitled "A Model of Balance of Payments Crises," written in 1977. It was a theoretical analysis of the reasons why attempts to maintain a fixed exchange rate typically end in abrupt speculative attacks, with billions of dollars of foreign exchange reserves lost in a matter of days or even hours. What I had in mind at the time were the attacks that brought down the Bretton Woods system in 1971 and its short-lived successor, the Smithsonian agreement, a year and a half later. It seemed to me then that the main interest of the paper would be historical; I did not expect to see attacks of that scale and drama again.

Based on a talk at the Group of 30, London, April 1997.

153

Luckily, I was wrong. I say "luckily," because as the founding father of what has long since become the academic industry of speculative attack theory, my citation index goes up every time another currency crisis materializes, trailing its tail of economic analyses and rationalizations. And the decade of the 1990s has so far produced a bumper crop of crises, which is fun for me if not for the ministers involved.

But why are there so many crises? Why haven't finance ministers, central bank governors, and so on learned to avoid them? To understand the durability of the speculative attack problem, you need to be aware of an underlying dilemma in exchange rate policy. To describe this dilemma, I find it helpful to think in terms of a little matrix of opinion, defined by the different answers to two questions.

The first question is whether flexibility on the exchange rate is useful. A country that fixes its exchange rate, in a world in which investors are free to move their money wherever they like, essentially gives up the opportunity to have its own monetary policy: Interest rates must be set at whatever level makes foreign exchange traders willing to keep the currency close to the target rate. A country that allows its exchange rate to float, on the other hand, can reduce interest rates to fight recessions, raise them to fight inflation. Is this extra freedom of policy useful, or is it merely illusory?

The second question is whether, having decided to float the currency, you can trust the foreign exchange market not to do anything crazy. Will the market set the currency at a value more or less consistent with the economy's fundamental strength and the soundness of the government's policies? Or will the market be subject to alternating bouts of irrational exuberance (to borrow Alan Greenspan's famous phrase) and unjustified pessimism?

The answers one might give to these questions define four boxes, all of which have their adherents. Here is the matrix:

|  |  | Is exchange rate flexibility useful? | |
|  |  | No | Yes |
| Can the forex market be trusted? | Yes | Relaxed guy | Serene floater |
|  | No | Determined fixer | Nervous wreck |

Suppose that you believe that the policy freedom a country gains from a floating exchange rate is actually worth very little, but you also trust the foreign exchange market not to do anything silly. Then you will be a very relaxed guy: You will not much care what regime is chosen for the exchange rate. You may have a small preference for a fixed rate or better yet a common currency, on the grounds that stable exchange rates reduce the costs of doing business; but you will not lose sleep over the choice. This is, I believe, the position of so-called "real business cycle" theorists, who believe as a matter of faith in the efficiency of private markets, and don't believe that monetary policies of any kind make much difference to how those markets function.

Suppose, on the other hand, that you believe that the freedom gained by floating is very valuable, but that financial markets can be trusted. Then you will be a serene floater: You will believe that freeing your currency from the shackles of a specific exchange rate target, so that you can get on with the business of pursuing full employment, is unambiguously a good thing. This was the view held by many economists in the late 1960s and early 1970s; indeed, I remember as an undergraduate picking up from my teachers a definite sense that they regarded the whole Bretton Woods system as a barbarous relic, a needless straitjacket on macroeconomic policy.

You will be equally sure of yourself if you believe the opposite: that foreign exchange markets are deeply unreliable, dominated by irrational bouts of optimism and pessimism, while the monetary freedom that comes with floating is of little value. You will then be a determined fixer, seeking to lash your currency immovably to the mast—best of all, by creating a common currency shared by as many countries as possible. This is, as I understand it, the position of most of the central bankers of continental Europe.

But what if you believe both that the freedom that comes from floating is valuable and that the markets that will determine your currency's value under floating are unreliable? Then you will be a nervous wreck, subject to stress-related disorders. You will regard any choice of currency regime as a choice between evils, and will always worry that you have chosen wrong.

Well, the last decade or so has given us a lot of evidence that bears on the two questions. True, the world rarely gives us clean natural experiments—although in some cases it comes pretty close. (For example, when Ireland decided in 1987 to stop pegging the punt to the pound sterling and start pegging it to the Deutsche mark, the prices of Irish goods abruptly stopped tracking the U.K. price level and starting following the German index instead—a fairly dramatic demonstration that money matters and therefore that monetary policy can matter, too, even in a small country.) I believe, however, that there is enough evidence to make a clear pronouncement: The nervous wrecks have it. Yes, the monetary freedom of a floating rate is valuable; no, the foreign exchange market cannot be trusted.

Let me start with the value of a floating rate. The classic case against there being any such value is that any attempt to make use of monetary autonomy will quickly backfire. Imagine, in particular, a country that drops its commitment to a fixed exchange rate, and uses that freedom to cut interest rates (which of course leads to a decline in the value of its currency). Ardent defenders of fixed rates insist that instead of an increase in employment, the result will very soon be a surge in inflation, wiping out both any gain in competiveness vis-à-vis foreign producers and any stimulus to real domestic demand. This was a position that seemed to be supported by a reading of the evidence in such cases as the repeated depreciations of the pound in the 1970s, or the devaluation of the Swedish krona in 1982.

To be honest, I never accepted that interpretation even of those events. But in any case a succession of more recent events has made it harder and harder to sustain this view of the way the world works. In the mid 1980s the U.S. dollar quickly dropped from 240 to 140 yen, from 3 marks to 1.8; there was not a hint of the surge in inflation that some had predicted. Many Europeans discounted this experience—after all, America, with its huge economy and relatively small reliance on international trade, is a special case; matters would be different if a European country tried the same thing. Then came the crises of 1992. I was assured by many French economists that Britain's departure from the Exchange Rate Mechanism would swiftly be punished; and Sweden's finance minister personally assured me that a depreciation of the krona would be an inflation disaster. Yet Britain got off scot-free—and even Sweden, when it depreciated a few weeks after my conversation with Ms. Wibble, suffered none of the predicted pain.

Nobody would claim that devaluing your currency is always and everywhere a good thing. What we can say, based on experience, is that the freedom to pursue an independent monetary policy that comes with a flexible exchange rate is indeed valuable as long as you start from a position of low inflation, and as long as domestic price increases are restrained by the presence of a lot of excess capacity. These may sound like restrictive conditions, but they aren't: They are exactly the conditions under which you would want the freedom to cut interest rates in the first place.

So far so good—but then there is the problem of the foreign exchange market.

Economists are, for understandable reasons, attached to the "efficient markets" theory of financial markets—a theory that attributes all fluctuations in financial prices to news about current or expected future fundamentals. As a sort of benchmark, an explanation of first resort for how asset prices behave, this theory has been enormously useful and productive—not to say lucrative, since much of the modern risk-management industry is based on that theory. But in many markets, very much including the foreign exchange market, the theory has become more or less impossible to believe as a literal description. Part of the argument involves technical tests—the anomalies just keep piling up, and the efforts to rationalize those anomalies within an efficient market framework have become an ever more desperate matter of adding epicycles.

But beyond these technical assessments, there is the simple question of plausibility—what it sometimes known as the "smell test." Can anyone come up with a good reason—which is to say real changes in what the markets knew about fundamentals—that justified a shift of the yen/dollar exchange rate from 120 plus in 1993, to 80 in 1995, then back to 120 plus in 1997? Isn't it far more reasonable to view the whole thing as a case of exchange traders following a trend they themselves had created? And of course these were not small swings: For Japanese industry the absurdly strong yen was a body blow.

So we are, as I said, firmly placed in the "nervous wreck" box of my little matrix. And that is the reason why the speculative attack industry—or perhaps I should say industries, since it comprises both those like me who write about such attacks, and, far more important, those like George Soros, who actually engage in them—continues to thrive.

After all, if ministers were serene floaters, they would simply treat the foreign exchange market with benign neglect; and they would therefore offer no target for speculative attack. If they were utterly determined fixers, they would do whatever was necessary to beat back speculative attacks—and the speculators, knowing this, would rarely attack in the first place. What creates an environment in which Soros can make money and I can write papers is the prevalence of finance ministers who decide to fix their currencies, but are suspected of being less than total in their commitment to that policy.

Let me say a bit more about the kind of speculative attacks that flourish in this environment; for there have been some major developments in the theory since I and a few other people started it twenty years ago.

The original models of such attacks imagined a country that was known to be following policies ultimately inconsistent with keeping its exchange rate fixed—for example, printing money to cover the budget deficit. That is, the eventual doom of the fixed rate was not in question to an informed observer. The speculative element came from the incentive of investors to anticipate the inevitable. Knowing that eventually the currency would drop in value, investors would try to get out of it in advance—but their very effort to get out of a weak currency would itself precipitate the collapse of the fixed rate. Understanding this, sophisticated investors would try to get out still earlier . . . the result was that a massive run on a currency could be expected at a time when it might still seem to have enough reserves to go on for many months or even years.

This analysis is still the canonical one, but recent discussion has emphasized three further concerns.

First, some economists have argued for the importance of self-fulfilling currency crises. They imagine a country whose government is prepared to pay the cost of sticking to an exchange rate indefinitely under ordinary circmstances, but which is not willing and/or able to put up with the pain of keeping interest rates high enough to support the currency in the face of speculators guessing that it might be devalued. In that case the fixed rate will survive if investors think it will; but it will also collapse if they think it will.

Second, there is the obvious point that if markets are subject to irrational shifts in opinion, to running with the herd, this applies as much to speculative attacks on fixed exchange rates as to gyrations in the value of flexible exchange rates. One remarkable fact is that there is not a sign in the markets that the great currency crises of the nineties were anticipated—that is, until only a few weeks before Black Wednesday in Britain, or the Mexican crisis of 1994, investors were cheerfully putting their money into pounds or pesos without demanding any exceptional risk premium. (This in spite of the fact that quite a few economists were actually warning in each case that a crisis might be in prospect). Then quite suddenly everyone wanted out. Was this because of some real news—other than the observation that everyone else suddenly wanted out?

Finally, there is the return of the gnomes of Zurich. Finance ministers whose currencies are under attack invariably blame their problems on the nefarious schemes of foreign market manipulators. Economists usually treat such claims with derision—after all, the British politician who coined the phrase was so ignorant that he didn't even know that the gnomes actually live in Basel. But nobody who has read a business magazine in the last few years can be unaware that these days there really are investors who not only move money in anticipation of a currency crisis, but actually do their best to trigger that crisis for fun and profit. These new actors on the scene do not yet have a standard name; my proposed term is "Soroi."

There are, of course, two ways to defeat all of these speculative pressures. One is to be basically indifferent to the exchange rate, depriving the Soroi of their "one-way option." The other is to lock in the exchange rate beyond all question—something best done by simply creating a common currency, leaving nothing to speculate in.

Which of these is the better solution? That is a peculiarly difficult question to answer. We have a theory of "optimum currency areas," which gives us a checklist of the things that ought to matter; but it is famously hard to turn that checklist into an operational set of criteria. What recent theorizing—backed by recent experience—does seem to indicate is that you should make a choice one way or the other. That is, in a world in which hot money can move as easily as it now does, an imperfectly credible fixed exchange rate combines the worst of both worlds: You forsake the policy freedom that comes with a flexible rate, yet you remain open to devastating speculative attacks.

If a group of countries decide that they should, in fact, adopt a common currency, everything we know about the economics says that they should follow what Barry Eichengreen calls the Nike strategy: Just do it. A prolonged transition period simply creates a target-rich environment for speculative attack, as markets have time to wonder, "Will they or won't they?"

One can only imagine the prospects for speculative havoc if the project to create a single currency involves a transition period of many years; sets rules for that transition period that impose severe economic hardship on the countries involved, hardship that undermines popular support for the project without in any real way preparing the ground for the unified currency; and last but not least, creates a basic uncertainty about whether any individual country, no matter how much it is committed to the idea of monetary union, will be allowed to join—because admission to the club is, in the end, contingent on criteria that are very hard to meet and in any case ambiguous in their interpretation.

Is it possible that the framers of the Maastricht Treaty—Europe's plan to create economic and monetary union—were secretly on the payroll of the Soroi? Or that they enjoyed the idea of playing a massive practical joke on their fellow Europeans? Or did they simply fail to think it through?

## Part 6

# Beyond the Market

*M*oney makes the economic world go round, but it is a means, not an end. The essays in this part of the collection are all, one way or another, about the difference between prices and values—and the light that economic analysis can shed on that difference.

The first, "Earth in the Balance Sheet," uses environmental politics to offer a new riff on an old theme in economics: the idea that markets go wrong when important scarce resources are *not* priced. The next pursues the same idea, this time focusing on traffic congestion. In both cases, the failures of markets offer a strong rationale for government intervention. Unfortunately, democratic politics itself is afflicted by some of the same "market failures" that the political process must try to cure; I address that problem in the third essay here, "Rat Democracy."

The remaining essays are less conventional in their themes. "A Medical Dilemma" argues that improvements in medical technology pose a deep moral and political issue: How much are we willing to let money buy? "The CPI and the Rat Race," taking off from some disputes about (of all things) the measurement of inflation, tries to get a grip on the implications of the indisputable fact that people care not only about how well they live in absolute terms, but about their relative status.

Finally, "Looking Backward" may need some explaining. It was written for a special centennial issue of the *New York Times Mag-*

*azine;* the assignment given to each of the authors was to write about his or her specialty as if looking back from the perspective of the year 2096. Incredibly, out of the fifteen or so authors only two were willing to play that game—the rest defied instructions and wrote boringly straight essays about "What I predict will happen over the next century." It's a mystery to me, because I thought the idea was great fun—although the essay is more serious than it looks.

# *Earth in the Balance Sheet: Economists Go for the Green*

Like most people who think at all about how much burden their way of life places on Spaceship Earth, I feel a bit guilty. But on Earth Day in 1997 my conscience was clearer than usual—and so were those of 2,500 other economists.

A few months earlier, an organization called Redefining Progress enlisted five economists—the Nobel laureates Robert Solow and Kenneth Arrow, together with Harvard's Dale Jorgenson, Yale's William Nordhaus, and myself—to circulate an "Econ-

Originally published in *Slate*, April 17, 1997.

omists' Statement on Climate Change," calling for serious measures to limit the emission of greenhouse gases. To be honest, I agreed to be one of the original signatories mainly as a gesture of goodwill, and never expected to hear any more about it; but the statement ended up being signed by, yes, more than 2,500 economists. Whatever else may come of the enterprise, it was an impressive demonstration of a little-known fact: Many economists are also enthusiastic environmentalists.

Partly this is just because of who economists are: Being by definition well-educated and, for the most part, pretty well-off, they have the usual prejudices of their class—and most upper-middle-class Americans are sentimental about the environment, as long as protecting it does not impinge on their lifestyle. (I bring bags and bottles to the recycling center in my gas-guzzling sports utility vehicle.) But my unscientific impression is that economists are on average more pro-environment than other people of similar incomes and backgrounds. Why? Because standard economic theory automatically predisposes those who believe in it to favor strong environmental protection.

This is not, of course, the popular image. Everyone knows that economists are people who know the price of everything and the value of nothing, who think that anything that increases gross domestic product is good and anything else is worthless, and who believe that whatever free markets do must be right. (I'm sorry to say that some of the people at Redefining Progress published an impressively ill-informed diatribe along these lines in the *Atlantic* back in 1995.)

But the reality is that even the most conventional economic doctrine is a lot more subtle than that. True, economists generally believe that a system of free markets is a pretty efficient way to run an economy, as long as the prices are right—as long, in particular, as people pay the true social cost of their actions. Environmental issues, however, more or less by definition involve situations in which the price is wrong—in which the private costs of an activity fail to reflect its true social costs. Let me quote from the textbook (by William Baumol and Alan Blinder) that I assigned when I taught Economics 1 last year: "When a firm pollutes a river, it uses some of society's resources just as surely as when it burns coal. However, if the firm pays for coal but not for the use of clean water, it is to be expected that management will be economical in its use of coal and wasteful in its use of water." In other words, when it comes to the environment, we do *not* expect the free market to get it right.

So what should be done? Going all the way back to Paul Samuelson's first edition in 1948, every economics textbook I know of has argued that the government should intervene in the market to discourage activities that damage the environment. The usual recommendation is to do so either by charging fees for the right to engage in such nasty activities—a.k.a. "pollution taxes"—or by auctioning off rights to pollute. Indeed, as the extraordinary response to the climate-change statement reminds us, the idea of pollution taxes is one of those iconic positions, like free trade, that commands the assent of virtually every card-carrying economist. Yet while pollution and related "negative externalities" such as traffic congestion are obvious problems, in practice, efforts to make markets take environmental costs into account are few and far between. So economists who actually believe the things they teach generally support a much more aggressive program of environmental protection than the one we actually have. True, they tend to oppose detailed regulations that tell people exactly how they must reduce pollution, preferring schemes that provide a financial incentive to pollute less but leave the details up to the private sector. But I would be hard pressed to think of a single economist not actually employed by an anti-environmental lobbying operation who believes that the United States should protect the environment less, not more, than it currently does. (The signers of the climate-change statement, incidentally, included thirteen economists from that temple of free-market theory, the University of Chicago.)

But won't protecting the environment reduce the gross domestic product? Not necessarily—and anyway, so what?

At first sight, it might seem obvious that pollution taxes will reduce GDP. After all, any tax reduces the incentives to work, save, and invest. Thus a tax on exhaust emissions from cars will induce people to drive cleaner cars or avoid driving altogether. But since it will also in effect lower the payoff to earning extra money (since you wouldn't end up driving the second car you could buy with that money anyway), people will not work as hard as they would have without the tax. The result is that taxes on pollution (or anything else) will, other things being equal, tend to reduce overall monetary output in the economy—which is to say, GDP.

But things need not be equal, because there is already a whole lot of taxing and spending going on. Even in the United States, where the government is smaller than in any other advanced country, about a third of GDP passes through its hands. So existing taxes already discourage people from engaging in taxable activities like working or investing. What this means is that the revenue from any new taxes on pollution could be used to reduce other taxes, such as Social Security contributions or the income tax (but not, of course, the capital-gains tax). While the pollution taxes would discourage some activities that are counted in the GDP, the reduction in other taxes would encourage other such activities. So measured GDP might well fall very little, or even rise.

Does this constitute an independent argument for taxing pollution, quite aside from its environmental payoff? Would we want to have, say, a carbon tax even if we weren't worried about global warming? Well, there has been an excruciatingly technical argument about this, mysteriously known as the "double dividend" debate; the general consensus seems to be no, and that on balance pollution taxes would be more likely to reduce GDP slightly than to increase it.

But so what? "Gross domestic product is not a measure of the nation's economic well-being"—so declares the textbook as soon as it introduces the concept. If getting the price of the environment right means a rise in consumption of nonmarket goods like clean air and leisure time at the expense of marketed consumption, so be it.

Isn't this amazing? Not only do thousands of economists agree on something, but what they agree on is the warm and cuddly idea that we should do more to protect the environment. Can 2,500 economists be wrong? Well, yes—but this time they aren't. The Great Green Tax Shift—a shift away from taxes on employment and income toward taxes on pollution and other negative externalities—has everything going for it. It is supported by good science and good economics, as well as by good intentions.

Inevitably, then, it appears at the moment to be a complete political nonstarter. The problem, as with many good policy ideas, is that the Great Green Tax Shift runs up against the three I's.

First, there is Ignorance. In 1996 Congress rushed to cut gasoline taxes to offset a temporary price rise. Not many voters stopped to ask where the money was coming from. So what politician will be foolish enough to take the first step in trying to institute new taxes on all-American pollution, even with the assurance that other taxes will be lowered at the same time? (My friends in the Clinton administration tell me that the word "taxes" has been banned even from internal discussions about environmental policy.)

Then there are Interests. It is hard to think of a way to limit global warming that will not gradually reduce the number of coal-mining jobs. As labor-market adjustment problems go, this is a pretty small one. But the coal miners and the energy companies are actively opposed to green taxes, while the broader public that would benefit from them is not actively in support.

Finally, there is Ideology. It used to be that the big problem in formulating a sensible environmental policy came from the Left—from people who insisted that since pollution is evil, it is immoral to put a price on it. These days, however, the main problem comes from the Right—from conservatives who, unlike most economists, really do think that the free market is always right—to such an extent that they refuse to believe even the most overwhelming scientific evidence if it seems to suggest a justification for government action.

So I do not, realistically, expect the Economists' Statement to change the world. But then I didn't expect it to go as far as it has. Certainly those of us who signed it did the right thing; and maybe, just maybe, we did our bit toward saving the planet.

# Taxes and Traffic Jams

**Why do we spend so much time talking about tax reform? Why don't we try to eliminate traffic jams instead?**

This is not a silly question. The case for doing something about traffic is based on impeccable free-market economics, every bit as solid as the argument for reforming our tax system. The difference is that whereas in practice tax reform is an iffy business—the plans currently being peddled would probably do more harm than

Originally published in *New York Times Magazine*, April 7, 1996. Copyright © 1996 by the New York Times Co. Reprinted by permission.

good—traffic reform is a $40 billion sure thing. The fact that traffic congestion, along with a number of similar issues like pollution management and water rights, goes unmentioned in current political discussion—and that when such issues do come up conservative politicians are often on the wrong side—tells you something important about the blinkered vision of many people who imagine that they are champions of free markets.

Let's talk for a moment about tax reform. The air is thick with schemes for flat taxes, value-added taxes, national sales taxes, and so on. Serious advocates of such proposals point out that the current system has two main flaws from the point of view of economic efficiency. First, some people pay a "marginal" tax rate as high as 40 percent—that is, of every extra dollar they earn forty cents goes to the I.R.S. This surely discourages people from working as hard as they might. Second, because the I.R.S. taxes interest and profits, the system discourages people from saving for the future. So theorists have devised alternative tax systems that might lead to greater work effort and higher savings, and might therefore expand the American economy.

But how big would these gains be? A lot of savings are already tax exempt, because of special tax breaks for retirement accounts. And we can't do away with taxes altogether: Like it or not, we still need to pay for the government services we want. This limits the scope for reducing marginal rates. For example: A realistic flat tax, one that would raise as much money as the current income tax, would still have to involve a marginal rate of well over 20 percent. That's lower than the 40 percent rate some people now pay, but most people don't pay that rate anyway. And even that twentysomething rate is possible only if we eliminate the tax deduction for interest on home mortgages—which means that while the economy might gain from the new tax, millions of middle-class families would lose.

The fact is that serious tax analysts believe that the net benefits from even a complete overhaul of the tax system would be modest, and that while most people might gain, many would lose. In practice, the prospect of middle-class outrage means that schemes like the flat tax are usually sold with the promise of unrealistically low tax rates. And while a realistic tax reform would be good for economic growth, the typical political scheme—which invariably promises to provide large tax cuts for the rich without any increases for the middle class, would create a massive budget deficit—thereby doing the economy far more harm than good.

Now let's talk about traffic. Traffic congestion is not a minor annoyance. Last year Americans lost more than eight billion hours to traffic delays, at a total economic cost of more than $80 billion—mainly in the form of wasted time, but also through extra consumption of gasoline, wear and tear on autos, and so on.

But aren't traffic jams just a fact of life? No: In large part they are the result of a system that, like the tax system, encourages people to make economically inefficient decisions.

Consider, for example, my own antisocial actions one day in 1996, when I was living and working at Stanford. A colleague who lived nearby and I were both going to a meeting in San Francisco, thirty miles away. At the cost of some minor inconvenience we could have traveled together. But we didn't, and by taking my own car I added marginally to the already world-class traffic congestion on Highway 101. I probably didn't delay any individual's morning commute by more than a fraction of a second—but that tiny delay was imposed on each of thousands of cars crawling along the freeway behind me. It's a good bet that the total delay that other people suffered for the sake of my slight convenience was more than an hour.

There ought to have been a way to make a deal: I wouldn't clog the freeway, and other drivers would compensate me for the inconvenience of carpooling. Since the cost I imposed on other people by driving during rush hour was much greater than the benefit I derived from so doing, such a deal could have made everyone happier. Of course it is impractical to make such a deal directly; but we can try to reproduce its results.

The classic economist's prescription for dealing with traffic is for the government to impose "congestion fees," tolls for using roads during periods of overcrowding. With modern technology such tolls could even be collected without tollbooths: An electronic sensor could pick up the signal from a tiny gizmo on your dashboard, or a low-powered laser could read a bar code on your windshield. The fees could then be rebated to the public. Realistic estimates suggest that such fees could cut the cost of traffic congestion dramatically, and leave the great majority of people better off. Most of those deterred from rush-hour driving would be more than compensated for their inconvenience through the rebate scheme. Those who continued to drive would be compensated for the extra tolls with a much faster trip to work.

I know what some conservative readers are thinking—that this is just another government intrusion into daily life. But think of it another way: What we have here is a problem of inadequately defined property rights. Space on Highway 101 during rush hour is a scarce resource, just like waterfront real estate. Unfortunately, nobody holds clear title to that resource, and so it gets overused.

So why don't we try to establish a properly functioning free market in road space? Suppose we issue every registered driver in a metropolitan area with a specified number of "rush hour points," which he is free to sell to other drivers at his discretion, and require anyone who drives during rush hour to present (electronically) the appropriate number of points. Let us also create a market in these points. Some people will continue to drive every day; they will need to purchase extra points. Others will find other ways of getting to work, and will sell their points for whatever price the, ahem, traffic will bear. How market-oriented can you get? And such a scheme, like congestion fees, will make most people better off—either because they get extra money by selling their points, or because the cost of buying points is more than offset by a quicker commute.

The reason creating a market in road space and imposing congestion fees would produce similar results is, of course, that—as any bright Econ 1 student can tell you—they are essentially equivalent. Either way, what you are doing is creating a market incentive for people like me to take into account the costs we impose on others by driving during rush hour.

The benefits of such a scheme would not be small change. Traffic experts tell us that a sensible system of congestion fees could easily cut the annual cost of traffic delays by $30 or 40 billion. Against these savings one must set the inconvenience to those who are deterred from driving; but the net benefits could be $15 billion a year or more. Add fees on heavy trucks that damage highways, and on air travel to crowded airports, and a middle-of-the-road estimate (and what other kind of estimate would you want?) is that traffic reform could enrich the American public by $40 to 50 billion every year.

There are other places where properly defined property rights could yield a big payoff. One example is water—a very scarce resource in the American West. Under the current system thirsty cities are rationed even while desert farmers feed irrigated alfalfa to their cattle. Why not create a free market in water rights? Another example is the airwaves, which used to carry only radio and television but are increasingly in demand to allow wireless communication among people and computers. Broadcast rights are now a valuable commodity, which could be traded in a free market, but—despite the recent auction of a limited slice of the spectrum—mostly aren't, with the result that bandwidth that could be carrying vital business data is carrying infomercials instead.

So why isn't there a major conservative politician out there campaigning on a platform of extending free-market principles, of creating property rights where they should exist but don't? Such a politician could promise to raise national income by $60, 80, even 100 billion a year—and he or she could do so honestly, without the slippery arithmetic that underlies the promises we are actually hearing.

To be fair, many conservative economists have advocated the kind of reforms I have described. (So have many liberal economists). But their voices have been completely ignored.

The reason, I believe, is that the political appeal of economic conservatism in the United States really has very little to do with an appreciation of the virtues of free markets. Instead it is about the promise of something for nothing—a rejection of the idea that taxes must be collected, that scarce resources must be conserved. The reason the electorate likes tax reform schemes is that they always end up being tax-cutting schemes, based on the premise that the voters pay taxes but someone else gets the benefits—even though anyone who looks at where the money actually goes quickly realizes that Pogo was right: We have met the enemy and they are us.

As a result, not only do prominent conservatives rarely support proposals to extend the range of the market; they often actively oppose them. For example, the supply-side guru George Gilder has campaigned vociferously against plans to auction off a limited slice of the airwaves. Instead, incredibly, he advocates anarchy—let anyone broadcast on whatever frequency he likes. This is crazy; what it reflects, one suspects, is a basic unwillingness to accept the idea that there are any scarce resources, any limits that must be respected.

So next time you encounter a conservative who likes to talk about the virtues of the free market, ask him what he thinks about creating a market in rights to drive in rush hour traffic, or to use Western water. If he demurs, then he doesn't really believe in free markets—he believes in free lunches. And all serious economists, whatever their politics, agree that there's no such thing.

# Rat Democracy

Like most people who once hoped for better, I have become resigned to the accumulation of tawdry detail about how President Clinton financed his reelection campaign. But condemning Clinton's brazen opportunism begs the question: Where did the opportunities to be so brazen come from?

This may seem to be a question for a political analyst, not an economist. But there is an approach to political analysis known as "rat choice" (rat as in "rational"—it's not a comment on the candidates) that flourishes along the border of the two fields. The working hypothesis of rat choice is that voting behavior reflects the more or less rational pursuit of individual interests. This may sound obvious, innocuous, and even excessively optimistic. But if you really think its implications through, they turn out to be quite subversive. Indeed, if you take rat choice seriously, you stop asking why democracy works so badly and start asking why it works at all.

What is the problem? Won't rational voters simply choose politicians who promise to serve their interests? Well, in a rough sense they do. The logic of democratic politics normally pushes both parties toward the center—more precisely, toward policies that serve the interests of the median voter. Consider, for example, the question of how big the government should be. In general, people with low incomes prefer a government that imposes high taxes in order to provide generous benefits. Those with high incomes prefer a government that does no such thing. The Democrats are, by inclination, the party of outstretched palms, the Republicans the party of tight fists. But both are forced to move away from those inclinations toward actual policies that more or less satisfy the voters in the middle, who don't like paying taxes but do like knowing that they won't be stuck with Grandma's medical bills.

But there are lots of issues that are not so big—issues that only involve, say, $10 or 20 billion a year—like who profits from electricity deregulation, or how much the government spends subsidizing irrigation water for Western farmers. Although these issues, cumulatively, are important to the electorate, the electorate doesn't vote—individual voters do. And it is rarely in the interest of the individual voter to take the trouble to track the details of public policy. After all, how much difference will one vote make?

Bells have just started going off in the head of any reader who remembers Econ 1. What I have just said is that the duties of a good citizen—such as becoming well informed before voting (and for that matter bothering to vote at all)—are subject to the dreaded *free-rider problem*. The free-rider problem arises whenever some valuable good or service is not "excludable"—that is, whenever the benefit cannot be restricted only to those who pay for it. It is clearly in the interest of all boaters to have a rescue service. But no individual boater has any incentive to pay for the service if others are willing to do so. If we leave provision of a lifesaving service up to individual decisions, each individual will try to free-ride on everyone else, and the service will be inadequate or worse.

The solution is government. It is in the collective interest of boaters that each boat owner be required to pay a fee, to support a Coast Guard that provides those nonexcludable benefits. And the same is true of police protection, public sanitation, national defense, the Centers for Disease Control, and so on. The free-rider problem is the most important reason all sane people concede that we need a government with some coercive power—the power, if nothing else, to force people to pay taxes whether or not they feel like it.

But there is a catch: The democratic process, the only decent way we know for deciding how that coercive power should be used, is itself subject to extremely severe free-rider problems. Rat-choice theorist Samuel Popkin writes (in his 1991 book, *The Reasoning Voter*): "Everybody's business is nobody's business. If everyone spends an additional hour evaluating the candidates, we all benefit from a better-informed electorate. If everyone but me spends the hour evaluating the candidates and I spend it choosing where to invest my savings, I will get a better return on my investments as well as a better government." As a result, the public at large is, entirely rationally, remarkably ill-informed about politics and policy. And that leaves the field open for special interests—which means people with a large stake in small issues—to buy policies that suit them.

For example, not many voters know or care whether the United States uses a substantial amount of its diplomatic capital to open European markets to Central American bananas. Why should they? (I only keep track of the dispute because I have to update my textbook, which includes the sentence: "Efforts to resolve Europe's banana split have proved fruitless.") But Carl Lindner, the corporate raider who now owns Chiquita Brands, has strong feelings about the issue; and thanks to his $500,000 in contributions, so does President Clinton. It's not that Clinton believed that money alone could buy him the election. But money does help, and any practical politician comes to realize that betraying the public interest on small issues involves little political cost, because voters lack the individual incentive to notice.

So what is the solution? One answer is to try to change the incentives of politicians, by making it more difficult for special interests to buy influence. It is easy to be cynical about this, but the truth is that legal limits on how money can be given do have considerable effect. To take only the most extreme example: Outright bribes do not, as far as we can tell, play a big role in determining federal policies—and who doubts that they would if they were legal? So by all means let us have campaign-finance reform; but let us not expect too much from it.

Another answer is to promote civic virtue. There are those who believe that if only the media would treat the public with proper respect, people would respond by acting responsibly—that they would turn away from salacious stories about celebrities and read earnest articles about the flat-panel-display initiative instead. Well, never mind. But it is probably true that the quality of politics in America has suffered from the erosion of public trust in institutions that used to act, to at least some degree, as watchdogs. Once upon a time a politician had to worry about the reactions of unions, churches, newspaper editors, even local political bosses, all of whom had the time and inclination to pay attention to politics beyond the sound bites. Now we have become an atomized society of individuals who get their news—if they get it at all—from TV. If anyone has a good idea about how to bring back the opinion leaders of yore, I am all for it.

Finally, we can try to remove temptation, by avoiding policy initiatives that make it easy for politicians to play favorites. This is one reason why some of us cringed when Ron Brown began taking planeloads of businessmen off on sales trips to China and so on. Whether or not those trips did any good, or gave the right impression about how foreigners might influence American foreign policy, they obviously raised the question of who got to be on the plane—and how.

But there is ultimately no way to make government by the people truly be government for the people. That is what rat choice teaches, and nobody has yet proved it wrong—even in theory.

# A Medical Dilemma

Back in the early 1980s, before the Internet had even been born, science-fiction writers like Bruce Sterling invented a genre that came to be known as "cyberpunk." Cyberpunk's protagonists were usually outlaw computer hackers, battling sinister multinational corporations for control of cyberspace (a term coined by another sci-fi novelist, William Gibson). But in his 1996 novel *Holy Fire*, Sterling imagines a rather different future: a world ruled by an all-powerful gerontocracy, which appropriates most of the world's wealth to pay for ever more costly life-extension techniques. And his heroine is, believe it or not, a ninety-four-year-old medical economist.

When the novel first came out, it seemed that Sterling was behind the curve. Public concern over medical costs peaked in 1993, then dropped off sharply. Not only did the Clinton health care plan crash and burn, the long-term upward trend in private medical costs also flattened, as corporations shifted many of their employees into cost-conscious HMOs. Even as debates over how to save Social Security make headlines, few question budget plans by both Congress and the Clinton administration that assume, while being systematically vague about the details, that the growth of Medicare can be sharply slowed with few ill effects. With remarkable speed, in other words, we have gone from a sense of crisis to a general belief that the problem of health costs will more or less take care of itself.

But recently there has been a flurry of stories with the ominous news that medical costs are on the rise again. Suddenly, our recent complacency about health costs looks as unjustified as our previous panic. In fact, both the panic and the complacency seem to stem from—what else?—a misdiagnosis of the nature of the problem.

Over the last generation the U.S. economy has been digitized; it has been globalized; but just as importantly, it has become medicalized. In 1970 we spent 7 percent of our GDP on medical care; today the number is twice that. Almost one worker in ten is employed in the health care service industry; if this trend continues, in a few years there will be more people working in doctors' offices and hospitals than in factories.

So what? As Harvard health economist Joseph Newhouse put it, "Neither citizens nor economists . . . are especially concerned about rapid growth in most sectors of the economy, like the personal computer industry, the fax industry, or the cellular phone industry." Yet where the growth of other industries is usually regarded as a cause for celebration, the growth of the medical sector is generally regarded as a bad thing. (Not long ago an article in the *Atlantic Monthly* even proposed a measure of economic growth that deducts health care from the GDP, on the grounds that medical expenditures are a cost, not a benefit.) Indeed, the very phrase "medical costs" seems to have the word "bloated" attached to it as a permanent modifier: We are not, everyone agrees, getting much for all that money.

Or are we? There is, of course, some truth to what Newhouse calls the "cocktail party story of excessive medical spending." Traditional medical insurance gives neither physicians nor their patients an incentive to think about costs; the result can be what health care reform advocate Alain Enthoven calls "flat of the curve" medicine, in which doctors order any procedure that might possibly be of medical value, no matter how expensive. Reintroducing some incentives can produce important savings. In 1983, for example, Medicare replaced its previous policy of paying all hospital costs with a new policy of paying hospitals a lump sum for any given procedure. The result was an immediate sharp drop in the average number of days in the hospital, with no apparent adverse medical effects.

But after that one-time saving, the cost of hospitalization began rising again. There is, in fact, a clear rhythm in the health care industry. Every once in a while there is a wave of cost-cutting moves—fixed fees for Medicare, replacing traditional insurance with HMOs—that slows the growth of medical expenses for a few years. But then the growth resumes.

Why can't we seem to keep the lid on medical costs? The answer—the clean little secret of health care—is simple: We actually do get something for our money. In fact, there is a consensus among health care experts that the main driving force behind ris-

ing costs is neither greed, nor inefficiency, nor even the aging of
our population, but technological progress. Medical expenditures
used to be small, not because doctors were cheap or hospitals were
well managed, but because there was only so much medicine had
to offer, no matter how much you were willing to spend. Since
the 1940s, however, every year has brought new medical advances:
new diagnostic techniques that can (at great expense) identify
problems that could previously only be guessed at; new surgical
procedures that can (at great expense) correct problems that could
previously only be allowed to take their course; new therapies that
can (at great expense) cure or at least alleviate conditions that
could previously only be endured. We spend ever more on medicine mainly because we keep on finding good new things that (a
lot of) money can buy.

It is often argued that the share of our national income that we
devote to health care cannot continue to rise in the future as it
has in the past. But why not? An old advertising slogan asserted
that "When you've got your health, you've got just about everything." Sterling's protagonist goes through an implausible procedure (albeit one based on an extrapolation of some real medical
research) that restores her youth; who would not give most of their
worldy goods for that? Even barring such medical miracles, it is
not hard to imagine that some day we might be willing to spend,
say, 30 percent of our income on treatments that prolong our lives
and improve their quality.

Some economists therefore argue that we should stop worrying about the rise in medical costs. By all means, they say, let us
encourage some economic rationality in the system—for example
by eliminating the bias created by the fact that wages are taxed
but medical benefits are not—but if people still want to spend an
ever-growing fraction of their income on health, so be it.

But matters are not quite that simple, for medicine is not just
like other goods.

The most direct difference between medicine and other things is that so much of it is paid for by the government. In most advanced countries the government pays for most medical care; even in free-market, antigovernment America, the public sector pays for more than 40 percent of medical expenditures. This in itself creates a special problem. It is not at all hard to see how the American economy could support a much larger medical sector; it is, however, very hard to see how the U.S. government will manage to pay for its share of that sector's costs. When Cassandras like Pete Peterson of the Concord Coalition present alarming numbers about the future burden of baby boomers on the budget, it turns out that only part of that prospective burden represents the sheer demographic effects of an aging population: Forecasts of rising medical costs account for the rest. Despite the aging of our population, the Congressional Budget Office projects that in 2030 Social Security payments will rise only from their current 5 percent of GDP to about 7 percent—but it projects that Medicare and Medicaid will rise from 4 to more than 10 percent of GDP. (Some people dismiss such forecasts: They point out that if medical costs were to rise to that extent, by the time baby boomers become a problem health care would be a much larger share of GDP than it is today—and that, they insist, is just not going to happen. But why not?)

Some might then say that the answer is obvious: We must abandon the idea that everyone is entitled to state-of-the-art medical care. (That is the hidden subtext of politicians who insist that Medicare is not being cut—that all that they are doing is slowing its growth). But are we really prepared to face up to the implications of such an abandonment?

We have come to take it for granted that in advanced nations almost everyone can at least afford the essentials of life. Ordinary people may not dine in three-star restaurants, but they have enough to eat; they may not wear Bruno Maglis, but they do not go barefoot; they may not live in Malibu, but they have a roof over their heads. Yet it was not always thus. In the past, the elite were physically superior to the masses, because only they had adequate nutrition: In the England of Charles Dickens, the adolescent sons of the upper class towered an average of four inches above their working-class contemporaries. What has happened since represents a literal levelling of the human condition, in a way that mere comparisons of the distribution of money income cannot capture.

There is really only one essential that is not within easy reach of the ordinary working American family, and that is medical care. But the rising cost of that essential—that is, the rising cost of buying the ever-growing list of useful things that doctors can now do for us—threatens to restore that ancient inequality with a vengeance.

Suppose that Lyndon Johnson had not passed Medicare in 1965. Then even now there would be a radical inequality in the prospects of the elderly rich and the ordinary citizen; the affluent would receive artificial hip replacements and coronary bypasses, while the rest would (like the elderly poor in less fortunate nations) limp along painfully—or die.

The current conventional wisdom is that the budget burden of health care will be cured with rationing—the Federal government will simply decline to pay for many of the expensive procedures that medical science makes available. But what if, as seems likely, those procedures really work—if there comes a time when those who can afford it can expect to be vigorous centenarians, and perhaps even buy themselves smarter children, while those who cannot can look forward only to the Biblical threescore and ten. Is this really a tolerable prospect?

There is, some might say, no alternative. But of course there is. It is possible to imagine a society that taxes itself heavily in order to provide advanced medical care to everyone, and that rations that care not by wealth but by other criteria. (Bruce Sterling's imaginary future is ruled by "the polity," a nanny state that rewards not wealth but personal hygiene: Society takes care of those who take care of themselves.)

Such an outcome sounds unthinkable in the current political climate, which is dominated by a low-tax, antigovernment ideology. But history is not over; ideologies may change. For all we know, the future may belong to the medical welfare state, a state whose slogan might be, "From each according to his ability, to each according to his needs."

# *The CPI and the Rat Race*

Let's talk about inflation indexing and the meaning of life.

Late in 1996 a panel of economists, led by Stanford's Michael Boskin, made semiofficial what most experts have been saying for some time: The Consumer Price Index overstates inflation. Nobody really knows by how much, but Boskin and company made a guesstimate of 1.1 percent annually. Compounded over decades, this is a huge error.

This conclusion is controversial. Some people are upset because

Originally published in *Slate*, December 21, 1996.

any reduction of inflation estimates will reduce Social Security benefits, which are indexed to the CPI. Others are upset because a revision of recent price history would mean abandoning a world-view on which they have staked their reputations. Quite a few people have committed themselves to the story line that productivity is up but real wages are down. If inflation has been lower than was previously assumed, that means the real value of wages may have gone up after all. And some economists with no particular ax to grind simply have doubts about the methodology.

Boskin may be right or wrong, but one argument by his critics is clearly wrong. They say, suppose it's true that inflation has been less than the official increase in the CPI over the past few decades. If you assume a lower inflation rate and recalculate real incomes back to, say, 1950, you reach what seems to be a crazy conclusion: That in the early 1950s, the era of postwar affluence, most Americans were living below what we now regard as the poverty line. Some critics of the Boskin report regard this as a decisive blow to its credibility.

The idea that most Americans were poor in 1950 is indeed absurd, but not because of Boskin's numbers. After all, even if you use an unadjusted CPI, the standard of living of the median family (fiftieth percentile) in 1950 America appears startlingly low by current standards. In that year, median-family income in 1994 dollars was only about $18,000. That's about the twentieth percentile today. Families at the twentieth percentile—that is, poorer than 80 percent of the population—may not be legally poor (only about 12 percent of families are officially below the poverty line), but they are likely to regard themselves as very disadvantaged and unsuccessful. So even using the old numbers, most families in 1950 had a material standard of living no better than that of today's poor or near-poor.

We can confirm this with more direct measures of the way people lived. In 1950 some 35 percent of dwellings lacked full indoor plumbing. Many families still did not have telephones or cars. And of course very few people had televisions. A modern American family at the twelfth percentile (that is, right at the poverty line) surely has a flushing toilet, a working shower, and a telephone with direct-dial long-distance service; probably has a color television; and may well even have a car. Take into account improvements in the quality of many other products, and it does not seem at all absurd to say that the material standard of living of that poverty-level family in 1996 is as good as or better than that of the median family in 1950.

What do we mean by this? We mean that if you could choose between the two material standards of living, other things being the same, you might well prefer the twelfth percentile standard of 1996 to the fiftieth percentile standard of 1950. But does that mean that most people were poor in 1950? No—because man does not live by bread, cars, televisions, or even plumbing alone.

Imagine that a mad scientist went back to 1950 and offered to transport the median family to the wondrous world of the 1990s, and to place them at, say, the twenty-fifth percentile level. The twenty-fifth percentile of 1996 is a clear material improvement over the median of 1950. Would they accept his offer? Almost surely not—because in 1950 they were middle class, while in 1996 they would be poor, even if they lived better in material terms. People don't just care about their absolute material level—they care about their level *compared with others*. 

I know quite a few academics who have nice houses, two cars, and enviable working conditions, yet are disappointed and bitter men—because they have never received an offer from Harvard and will probably not get a Nobel Prize. They live very well in material terms, but they judge themselves relative to their reference group, and so they feel deprived. And on the other hand, it is an open secret that the chief payoff from being really rich is, as Tom Wolfe once put it, the pleasure of "seeing 'em jump." Privilege is not merely a means to other ends, it is an end in itself.

My fellow *Slate* columnist Robert Wright would undoubtedly emphasize that our concern over status exists for good evolutionary reasons. In the ancestral environment a man would be likely to have more offspring if he got his pick of the most fertile-seeming women. That, in turn, would depend on his status, not his absolute standard of living. So males with a predisposition to status-seeking left more offspring than those without, and the end result is Bill G-g-g—I mean, Ronald Perelman.

Is my license as a practicing economist about to be revoked? Aren't we supposed to believe in Economic Man? And doesn't admitting that people care about fuzzy things like status undermine the whole economic method? Not really: Homo economicus is not a central pillar of my faith—he is merely a working assumption, albeit one that is extremely useful in many circumstances.

But admitting that people's happiness depends on their relative economic level as well as their absolute economic resources has some subversive implications. For example: Many conservatives have seized on the Boskin report as a club with which to beat all those liberals who have been whining about declining incomes and increasing poverty in America. It was all, they insist, a statistical hoax. But you could very well make the opposite argument. America in the 1950s was a middle-class society in a way that America in the 1990s is not. That is, it had a much flatter income distribution, so that people had much more sense of sharing a common national lifestyle. And people in that relatively equal America felt good about their lives, even though by modern standards, they were poor—poorer, if Boskin is correct, than we previously thought. Doesn't this mean, then, that having a more or less equal distribution of income makes for a happier society, even if it does not raise anyone's material standard of living? That is, you can use the fact that people did not feel poor in the 1950s as an argument for a more radical egalitarianism than even most leftists would be willing to espouse.

You could even argue that American society in the 1990s is an engine that maximizes achievement yet minimizes satisfaction. In a society with a very flat distribution of income and status, nobody feels left out. In a society with rigid ranks, people do not expect to rise above their station and therefore do not feel that they have failed if they do not rise. (Aristocrats are not part of a peasant's reference group.) Modern America, however, is a hugely unequal society in which anyone can achieve awesome success, but not many actually do. The result is that many—perhaps even most—people feel that they have failed to make the cut, no matter how comfortable their lives. (In a land where anyone can become president, anyone who *doesn't* become president is a failure.) My European friends always marvel at how hard Americans work, even those who already have plenty of money. Why don't we take more time to enjoy what we have? The answer, of course, is that we work so hard because we are determined to get ahead—an effort that (for Americans as a society) is doomed to failure, because competition for status is a zero-sum game. We can't all "get ahead." No matter how fast we all run, someone must be behind.

If one follows this line of thought one might well be led to some extremely radical ideas about economic policy, ideas that are completely at odds with all current orthodoxies. But I won't try to come to grips with such ideas in this column. Frankly, I don't have the time. I have to get back to my research—otherwise, somebody else might get that Nobel.

# Looking Backward

When looking backward, one must always be prepared to make allowances: It is unfair to blame late twentieth-century observers for their failure to foresee everything about the century to come. Long-term social forecasting is an inexact science even now, and in 1996 the founders of modern nonlinear socioeconomics were still obscure graduate students. Still, even then many people understood that the major forces driving economic change would be

Originally published in *New York Times Magazine*, September 29, 1996, under the title "White Collars Turn Blue." Copyright © 1996 by the New York Times Co. Reprinted by permission.

the continuing advance of digital technology, on one side, and the spread of economic development to previously backward nations, on the other; in that sense there were no big surprises. The puzzle is why the pundits of the time completely misjudged the consequences of those changes.

Perhaps the best way to describe the flawed vision of fin-de-siècle futurists is to say that, with few exceptions, they expected the coming of an "immaculate" economy—an economy in which people would be largely emancipated from any grubby involvement with the physical world. The future, everyone insisted, would bring an "information economy," which would mainly produce intangibles; the good jobs would go to "symbolic analysts," who would push icons around on computer screens; and knowledge rather than traditionally important resources like oil or land would become the main source of wealth and power.

But even in 1996 it should have been obvious that this was silly. First, for all the talk of an information economy, ultimately an economy must serve consumers—and consumers don't want information, they want tangible goods. In particular, the billions of Third World families who finally began to have some purchasing power as the twentieth century ended did not want to watch pretty graphics on the Internet—they wanted to live in nice houses, drive cars, and eat meat. Second, the Information Revolution of the late twentieth century was—as everyone should have realized—a spectacular but only partial success. Simple information processing became faster and cheaper than anyone had imagined possible; but the once confident Artificial Intelligence movement went from defeat to defeat. As Marvin Minsky, one of the movement's founders, despairingly remarked, "What people vaguely call common sense is actually more intricate than most of the technical expertise we admire." And it takes common sense to deal with the physical world—which is why, even at the end of the twenty-first century, there are still no robot plumbers.

Most important of all, the prophets of an "information economy" seem to have forgotten basic economics. When something becomes abundant, it also becomes cheap. A world awash in information will be a world in which information per se has very little market value. And in general when the economy becomes extremely good at doing something, that activity becomes less rather than more important. Late-twentieth-century America was supremely efficient at growing food; that was why it had hardly any farmers. Late-twenty-first-century America is supremely efficient at processing routine information; that is why the traditional white-collar worker has virtually disappeared from the scene.

With these observations as background, then, let us turn to the five great economic trends that observers in 1996 should have expected but didn't.

*Soaring resource prices.* The first half of the 1990s was an era of extraordinarily low raw-material prices. Yet it is hard to see why anyone thought this situation would continue. The Earth is, as a few lonely voices continued to insist, a finite planet; when two billion Asians began to aspire to Western levels of consumption, it was inevitable that they would set off a scramble for limited supplies of minerals, fossil fuels, and even food.

In fact, there were some warning signs as early as 1996. There was a temporary surge in gasoline prices during the spring of that year, due to an unusually cold winter and miscalculations about Middle East oil supplies. Although prices soon subsided, the episode should have reminded people that by the mid-nineties the world's industrial nations were once again as vulnerable to disruptions of oil supply as they had been in the early 1970s; but the warning was ignored.

Quite soon, however, it became clear that natural resources, far from becoming irrelevant, had become more crucial than ever before. In the nineteenth century great fortunes were made in industry; in the late twentieth they were made in technology; but today's superrich are, more often than not, those who own prime land or mineral rights.

*The environment as property.* In the twentieth century people used some quaint expressions—"free as air," "spending money like water"—as if such things as air and water were available in unlimited supply. But in a world where billions of people have enough money to buy cars, take vacations, and buy food in plastic packages, the limited carrying capacity of the environment has become perhaps the single most important constraint on the average standard of living.

By 1996 it was already clear that one way to cope with environmental limits was to use the market mechanism—in effect to convert those limits into new forms of property rights. A first step in this direction was taken in the early 1990s, when the U.S. government began allowing electric utilities to buy and sell rights to emit certain kinds of pollution; the principle was extended in 1995 when the government began auctioning off rights to use the electromagnetic spectrum. Today, of course, practically every activity with an adverse impact on the environment carries a hefty price tag. It is hard to believe that as late as 1995 an ordinary family could fill up a Winnebago with dollar-a-gallon gasoline, then pay only five dollars to drive it into Yosemite. Today such a trip would cost about fifteen times as much even after adjusting for inflation.

The economic consequences of the conversion of environmental limits into property were unexpected. Once governments got serious about making people pay for the pollution and congestion they caused, the cost of environmental licenses became a major part of the cost of doing business. Today license fees account for more than 30 percent of GDP. And such fees have become the main source of government revenue; after repeated reductions, the Federal income tax was finally abolished in 2043.

*The rebirth of the big city.* During the second half of the twentieth century, the traditional densely populated, high-rise city seemed to be in unstoppable decline. Modern telecommunications had eliminated much of the need for close physical proximity between routine office workers, leading more and more companies to shift their backoffice operations from lower Manhattan and other central business districts to suburban office parks. It began to seem as if cities as we knew them would vanish, replaced with an endless low-rise sprawl punctuated by an occasional cluster of ten-story office towers.

But this proved to be a transitory phase. For one thing, high gasoline prices and the cost of environmental permits made a one-person, one-car commuting pattern impractical. Today the roads belong mainly to hordes of share-a-ride minivans, efficiently routed by a web of intercommunicating computers. However, although this semi-mass-transit system works better than twentieth-century commuters could have imagined—and employs more than four million drivers—suburban door-to-door transportation still takes considerably longer than it did when ordinary commuters and shoppers could afford to drive their own cars. Moreover, the jobs that had temporarily flourished in the suburbs—mainly relatively routine office work—were precisely the jobs that were eliminated in vast numbers beginning in the mid-nineties. Some white-collar jobs migrated to low-wage countries; others were taken over by computers. The jobs that could not be shipped abroad or handled by machines were those that required the human touch—that required face-to-face interaction, or close physical proximity between people working directly with physical materials. In short, they were jobs best done in the middle of dense urban areas, areas served by what is still the most effective mass-transit system yet devised: the elevator.

Here again, there were straws in the wind. At the beginning of the 1990s, there was much speculation about which region would become the center of the burgeoning multimedia industry. Would it be Silicon Valley? Los Angeles? By 1996 the answer was clear; the winner was . . . Manhattan, whose urban density favored the kind of close, face-to-face interaction that turned out to be essential. Today, of course, Manhattan boasts almost as many 200-story buildings as St. Petersburg or Bangalore.

*The devaluation of higher education.* In the 1990s everyone believed that education was the key to economic success, for both individuals and nations. A college degree, maybe even a postgraduate degree, was essential for anyone who wanted a good job as one of those "symbolic analysts."

But computers are very good at analyzing symbols; it's the messiness of the real world they have trouble with. Furthermore, symbols can be quite easily transmitted to Asmara or La Paz and analyzed there for a fraction of the cost of doing it in Boston. So over the course of this century many of the jobs that used to require a college degree have been eliminated, while many of the rest can, it turns out, be done quite well by an intelligent person whether or not she has studied world literature.

This trend should have been obvious even in 1996. After all, even then America's richest man was Bill Gates, a college dropout who didn't seem to need a lot of formal education to build the world's most powerful information technology company.

Or consider the panic over "downsizing" that gripped America in 1996. As economists quickly pointed out, the rate at which Americans were losing jobs in the nineties was not especially high by historical standards. Why, then, did downsizing suddenly become news? Because for the first time white-collar, college-educated workers were being fired in large numbers, even while skilled machinists and other blue-collar workers were in high demand. This should have been a clear signal that the days of ever-rising wage premia for people with higher education were over, but somehow nobody noticed.

Eventually, of course, the eroding payoff to higher education created a crisis in the education industry itself. Why should a student put herself through four years of college and several years of postgraduate work in order to acquire academic credentials with hardly any monetary value? These days jobs that require only six or twelve months of vocational training—paranursing, carpentry, household maintenance (a profession that has taken over much of the housework that used to be done by unpaid spouses), and so on—pay nearly as much as one can expect to earn with a master's degree, and more than one can expect to earn with a Ph.D. And so enrollment in colleges and universities has dropped almost two-thirds since its turn-of-the-century peak. Many institutions of higher education could not survive this harsher environment. The famous universities mostly did manage to cope, but only by changing their character and reverting to an older role. Today a place like Harvard is, as it was in the nineteenth century, more of a social institution than a scholarly one—a place for the children of the wealthy to refine their social graces and make friends with others of the same class.

*The celebrity economy.* The last of this century's great trends was noted by acute observers in 1996, yet somehow most people failed to appreciate it. Although business gurus were proclaiming the predominance of creativity and innovation over mere routine production, in fact the growing ease with which information could be transmitted and reproduced was making it ever harder for creators to profit from their creations. Today, if you develop a marvelous piece of software, by tomorrow everyone will have downloaded a free copy from the Net. If you record a magnificent concert, next week bootleg CDs will be selling in Shanghai. If you produce a wonderful film, next month high-quality videos will be available in Mexico City.

How, then, can creativity be made to pay? The answer was already becoming apparent a century ago: Creations must make money indirectly, by promoting sales of something else. Just as auto companies used to sponsor Grand Prix racers to spice up the image of their cars, computer manufacturers now sponsor hotshot software designers to build brand recognition for their hardware. And the same is true for individuals. The royalties the Four Sopranos earn from their recordings are surprisingly small; mainly the recordings serve as advertisements for their arena concerts. The fans, of course, go to these concerts not to appreciate the music (they can do that far better at home) but for the experience of seeing their idols in person. Technology forecaster Esther Dyson got it precisely right in 1996: "Free copies of content are going to be what you use to establish your fame. Then you go out and milk it." In short, instead of becoming a Knowledge Economy we have become a Celebrity Economy.

Luckily, the same technology that has made it impossible to capitalize directly on knowledge has also created many more opportunities for celebrity. The 500-channel world is a place of many subcultures, each with its own culture heroes; there are people who will pay for the thrill of live encounters not only with divas but with journalists, poets, mathematicians, and even economists. When Andy Warhol predicted a world in which everyone would be famous for fifteen minutes, he was wrong: If there are indeed an astonishing number of people who have experienced celebrity, it is not because fame is fleeting but because there are many ways to be famous in a society that has become incredibly diverse.

Still, the celebrity economy has been hard on some people—especially those of us with a scholarly bent. A century ago it was actually possible to make a living as a more or less pure scholar: Someone like myself would probably have earned a pretty good salary as a college professor, and been able to supplement that income with textbook royalties. Today, however, teaching jobs are hard to find and pay a pittance in any case; and nobody makes money by selling books. If you want to devote yourself to scholarship, there are now only three options (the same options that were available in the nineteenth century, before the rise of institutionalized academic research). Like Charles Darwin, you can be born rich, and live off your inheritance. Like Alfred Wallace, the less fortunate co-discoverer of evolution, you can make your living doing something else, and pursue research as a hobby. Or, like many nineteenth-century scientists, you can try to cash in on scholarly reputation by going on the paid lecture circuit.

But celebrity, though more common than ever before, still does not come easily. And that is why writing this article is such an opportunity. I actually don't mind my day job in the veterinary clinic, but I have always wanted to be a full-time economist; an article like this might be just what I need to make my dream come true.

# READ MORE IN PENGUIN

In every corner of the world, on every subject under the sun, Penguin represents quality and variety – the very best in publishing today.

For complete information about books available from Penguin – including Puffins, Penguin Classics and Arkana – and how to order them, write to us at the appropriate address below. Please note that for copyright reasons the selection of books varies from country to country.

**In the United Kingdom:** Please write to *Dept. EP, Penguin Books Ltd, Bath Road, Harmondsworth, West Drayton, Middlesex UB7 ODA*

**In the United States:** Please write to *Consumer Sales, Penguin Putnam Inc., P.O. Box 12289 Dept. B, Newark, New Jersey 07101-5289.* VISA and MasterCard holders call 1-800-788-6262 to order Penguin titles

**In Canada:** Please write to *Penguin Books Canada Ltd, 10 Alcorn Avenue, Suite 300, Toronto, Ontario M4V 3B2*

**In Australia:** Please write to *Penguin Books Australia Ltd, P.O. Box 257, Ringwood, Victoria 3134*

**In New Zealand:** Please write to *Penguin Books (NZ) Ltd, Private Bag 102902, North Shore Mail Centre, Auckland 10*

**In India:** Please write to *Penguin Books India Pvt Ltd, 11 Community Centre, Panchsheel Park, New Delhi 110017*

**In the Netherlands:** Please write to *Penguin Books Netherlands bv, Postbus 3507, NL-1001 AH Amsterdam*

**In Germany:** Please write to *Penguin Books Deutschland GmbH, Metzlerstrasse 26, 60594 Frankfurt am Main*

**In Spain:** Please write to *Penguin Books S. A., Bravo Murillo 19, 1° B, 28015 Madrid*

**In Italy:** Please write to *Penguin Italia s.r.l., Via Benedetto Croce 2, 20094 Corsico, Milano*

**In France:** Please write to *Penguin France, Le Carré Wilson, 62 rue Benjamin Baillaud, 31500 Toulouse*

**In Japan:** Please write to *Penguin Books Japan Ltd, Kaneko Building, 2-3-25 Koraku, Bunkyo-Ku, Tokyo 112*

**In South Africa:** Please write to *Penguin Books South Africa (Pty) Ltd, Private Bag X14, Parkview, 2122 Johannesburg*

# READ MORE IN PENGUIN

## BUSINESS AND ECONOMICS

**Webonomics**  Evan I. Schwartz

In *Webonomics*, Evan I. Schwartz defines nine essential principles for growing your business on the Web. Using case studies of corporations such as IBM and Volvo, as well as smaller companies and web-based start-ups, Schwartz documents both the tremendous failures and the successes on the Web in a multitude of industries.

**Inside Organizations**  Charles B. Handy

Whatever we do, whatever our profession, organizing is a part of our lives. This book brings together twenty-one ideas which show you how to work with and through other people. There are also questions at the end of each chapter to get you thinking on your own and in a group.

**Lloyds Bank Small Business Guide**  Sara Williams

This long-running guide to making a success of your small business deals with real issues in a practical way. 'As comprehensive an introduction to setting up a business as anyone could need' *Daily Telegraph*

**Teach Yourself to Think**  Edward de Bono

Edward de Bono's masterly book offers a structure that broadens our ability to respond to and cope with a vast range of situations. *Teach Yourself to Think* is software for the brain, turning it into a successful thinking mechanism, and, as such, will prove of immense value to us all.

**The Road Ahead**  Bill Gates

Bill Gates – the man who built Microsoft – takes us back to when he dropped out of Harvard to start his own software company and discusses how we stand on the brink of a new technology revolution that will for ever change and enhance the way we buy, work, learn and communicate with each other.